Praise for *God, ...*

Rev. Dr. Driver peels back layers of the Genesis stories of faith that we know, to explore them in new and thought-provoking ways. As the stories come alive, he names the family traumas in such a way that the reader joins the story of Scripture, naming evil and the sins of patriarchy, racism, and sexism. Especially insightful are the implications for ministry. These insights are ways the church can see past the surface story and see people as people, support victims of abuse, and be a beacon of hope that God, in Jesus Christ, is with us even in the pain and suffering of life. Thank you for making this real.

—Suzanne Darcy Dillahunt, bishop, Southern Ohio Synod, Evangelical Lutheran Church in America

Driver's insightful work provides a fresh perspective on Scripture for those affected by trauma, particularly survivors of gender-based violence. This book offers a compassionate alternative to traditional patriarchal interpretations of Genesis, challenging shame-based beliefs often reinforced by such readings. While acknowledging that some survivors may choose to distance themselves from biblical texts, Driver creates a thoughtful and gentle pathway for those seeking to reengage with Scripture. This valuable resource serves as a healing balm for readers navigating the complex intersection of faith and trauma recovery.

—Hannah Estabrook, MA, LPCC-S, executive director of Sanctuary Night, and author of *Freedom to Heal: A Christian Clinician's Guide to Treating Child Sexual Abuse*

In this crucial book, Cory Driver explores the traumatic experiences of biblical individuals and families with compassion, careful attention, and astute insight that offer wisdom and hope for those who have had their own traumatic experiences and those who accompany and care for them. Along the way, Driver brings the ancient and ever-new

Jewish practice of midrash into living engagement with biblical scholarship and lived human experience to bring biblical stories and their characters to life in new, oft-troubling, and graciously redemptive ways.
—William O. Gafkjen, bishop, Indiana-Kentucky Synod, Evangelical Lutheran Church in America

This is a book that "says the quiet part out loud," courageously naming the sexual trauma that pervades the experiences of characters in the book of Genesis. It can be deeply disconcerting to read these texts through the lens of trauma, but Driver does not leave his readers to despair. Instead, he helps us to turn both the horror and the hope of these sacred stories toward the healing of wounds in our communities.
—Cameron B. R. Howard, associate professor of Old Testament, Luther Seminary

Informed by rabbinic and modern biblical interpretation, Cory Driver offers careful and original readings of several biblical stories related to gender-based and sexual trauma. Driver reads these texts with thoughtfulness and compassion and proposes pastorally sensitive lessons to be learned from them. Undergirding his readings is the affirmation that "the Lord is close to the brokenhearted, and saves those who are crushed in spirit" (Psalm 34:18). This book will be valuable both for those who have suffered such trauma and for those who care for them.
—Kathryn Schifferdecker, professor and Elva B. Lovell Chair of Old Testament, Luther Seminary

GOD, GENDER, AND FAMILY TRAUMA

GOD, GENDER, AND FAMILY TRAUMA

HOW REREADING GENESIS CAN BE A REVELATION

Cory Pechan Driver

Fortress Press
Minneapolis

GOD, GENDER, AND FAMILY TRAUMA
How Rereading Genesis Can Be a Revelation

Copyright © 2025 Fortress Press. All rights reserved. Except for brief quotations in critical articles and reviews, no part of this book may be reproduced in any manner without prior written permission from the publisher. Email copyright@fortresspress.com or write to Permissions, Fortress Press, Box 1209, Minneapolis, MN 55440-1209.

30 29 28 27 26 25   1 2 3 4 5 6 7 8 9

Unless otherwise noted, all Scripture quotations are taken from New American Standard Bible®, Copyright © 1960, 1971, 1977, 1995, 2020 by The Lockman Foundation. All rights reserved.

Scripture quotations marked KJV are taken from King James Version. Public domain.

Library of Congress Cataloging-in-Publication Data

Names: Driver, Cory Thomas Pechan, author.
Title: God, gender, and family trauma : how rereading Genesis can be a revelation / Cory Pechan Driver.
Description: Minneapolis : Fortress Press, [2025] | Includes bibliographical references and index.
Identifiers: LCCN 2024020680 (print) | LCCN 2024020681 (ebook) | ISBN 9798889832201 (print) | ISBN 9798889832218 (ebook)
Subjects: LCSH: Gender identity in the Bible. | Sex role—Biblical teaching. | Families—Biblical teaching. | Families—Mental health. | Bible. Genesis—Social scientific criticism.
Classification: LCC BS1199.G36 D75 2025 (print) | LCC BS1199.G36 (ebook) | DDC 222/.11083053—dc23/eng/20240708
LC record available at https://lccn.loc.gov/2024020680
LC ebook record available at https://lccn.loc.gov/2024020681

Cover design and illustration: Kristin Miller

Print ISBN: 979-8-8898-3220-1
eBook ISBN: 979-8-8898-3221-8

For G., N., and R.
you are my loves

CONTENTS

Acknowledgments ix

Introduction 1
1. Learning to Read 9
2. Gender Bias and Other Problems 29
3. Disguise and Authenticity 45
4. Holding Space and Recognizing Agency 71
5. The Trauma of Job's Wife 89
6. Survivors Fighting for Justice 101
7. Pathways to Resistance and Freedom 119

Bibliography 139
Index 145

ACKNOWLEDGMENTS

This work, more than anything else that I have ever created, has taken a village. Professors Amy Marga, Beverly Wallace, Cameron Howard, and Kathryn Schifferdecker all read early versions of these chapters and provided helpful feedback and encouragement. Kathryn especially has been a committed friend, mentor, and supporter throughout the process. My faithful circle of early editors gave gracious feedback and improved my work immeasurably. Monica Burt, Hannah Estabrook, and Jennifer Sheek were generous with their time and their wisdom. Laura Gifford at Fortress Press believed in the work, and you are holding it today because of her kindness. The students, staff, and faculty of the Evangelical Theological Seminary in Cairo were important conversation partners during the writing of this work. I am grateful that we shared our lives, even if all too briefly. More than anyone, I want to thank my partner and wife, Sarah, for living the daily truth that justice is healing, and healing is justice.

INTRODUCTION

*The LORD is near to the brokenhearted
And saves those who are crushed in spirit.*

—Psalm 34:18

AT THE VERY beginning of a book about gendered and sexual trauma and healing in the Bible, the good news is that God sees and knows that people are sometimes brokenhearted and crushed in spirit. The even better news is that God is intimately present with those going through traumatic events and saves those suffering in the aftermath of trauma. The best news, in the words of pastor and trauma therapist Hannah Estabrook, is that God uses humans—Jesus's body on earth—to provide intimacy and healing care for folks who have experienced trauma in their lives. We are to be close to the brokenhearted because God is. Trauma-informed care is the work of the whole body of Christ.

But where do we start? We start by getting curious. We start by asking ourselves and our communities, What parts of our stories—especially the parts we are uncomfortable sharing—are affecting us now? How have the traumatic parts of our pasts (or present) shaped our lives, individually and communally? What deep, unhealed hurts are affecting our physical, emotional, and spiritual selves?

We must not simply wade into the murky present and attempt to change problematic or strange behaviors. We must learn people's stories. We must earn trust to hear and hold the messy, icky, confusing, painful parts of stories. And we must keep returning to the stories behind the stories. When we remember, we must re-member; that is, we must put stories and selves back together from the ways that they have been dis-membered. All too often, our stories and lives have been parsed, abbreviated, and suppressed in ways that allow for the hiding or ignoring of difficult truths. This is why we turn to Genesis for stories that will not be hidden.

We know the stories of Abraham and Sarah going to a new land. We know the story of Jacob tricking his brother and father out of a blessing. And we know the story of Joseph and his colorful garment. But what are the stories behind those stories? How do these stories and the painful trauma within them reverberate across the generations? Was Sarah's story a journey of faithfulness or of dehumanization? Was Jacob really a trickster, or was he a pawn in a game played by others? What can we learn about Joseph's understanding of himself by his changing garments throughout his life? We must pay attention to these details. We must ask what stories we have allowed ourselves to skip over or ignore because they are uncomfortable or cast the characters we love in a bad light.

This work of trauma-informed Bible study is important for (at least) four reasons. The first is that it honors the trauma survivors in the midst of the community. If we preach on Jacob, Rachel, and Leah but do not address how both the sisters (and their servants!) felt unloved and unvalued for much of their lives, we are missing a crucial opportunity to practice the empathetic closeness that God desires for those experiencing emotional trauma in their own relationships. Scripture, and especially the patriarchal narratives of Genesis, are full of accounts of survivors—and victims—of gendered and sexual trauma. These stories can be a source of inspiration, hope, strength, and ultimately recognition for people experiencing trauma in their own lives. Just as God was with Jacob, Leah, and Rachel as they all abused and were abused by each other, God is with those living through abuse in the present. These are our stories, if only we have eyes to see them.

Second, trauma-informed biblical interpretation helps us mature in our reading of Scripture. By delving richly into the text, we can become reacquainted with spiritual ancestors and see them in a new, more honest light. Abraham was a paragon of faithful following of God. But he also traumatized his wife, alienated his son, and abused his second wife and her son—consigning them to near-death in the wilderness. Abraham, Sarah, Jacob, Judah, and Joseph must not be unquestioned idols for us but rather full humans, capable of great acts of faith but also great acts of cruelty. Seeing the fullness of potential, for good and for ill, in the biblical characters helps train us to be willing to look past sheltering silences in our families and communities and honestly take stock of the traumatic stories that have been regarded as unmentionable for far too long.

Third, reading with a trauma-informed lens helps us mature in understanding the overlapping and intersecting layers of human identity. The experience of Joseph as an enslaved foreign man in Egypt was in some ways quite like the experience of HaGar,[1] an enslaved foreign woman in Hebrew contexts. And yet, their experiences differ in profoundly important ways as well. Joseph said and did things that HaGar could not, and vice versa. Mature, trauma-informed reading will discern repeated patterns of abuse—and healing—while taking seriously the ways that intersectional identities shape the particular experiences of victims and survivors.[2]

Fourth, and most importantly, practicing trauma-informed interpretation is a loving and relatively safe way to sharpen skills of trauma-informed care for the people in our midst. If we miss the suffering of Sarah, Hagar, Dinah, Leah, Rachel, or Tamar in our first hundred—or thousand—readings of their stories, they are not offended or hurt. However, if we repeatedly miss cuing into the suffering of our neighbor, whose pain comes out in stories that we hear with our own ears, we miss the chance to love a living human. Put bluntly, we

---

1. I explain the spelling, and especially the capital *G*, in chapter 1.

2. Intersectionality, a term coined by Kimberlé Crenshaw in 1989, explores the ways that social and political identities overlap and influence each other in generating potential privilege and discrimination.

practice trauma-informed reading of stories of Scripture overflowing with generational sexual and gender trauma so that we can be better equipped to recognize trauma in those around us—and in ourselves.

Now, not all of us are going to earn master's degrees in counseling or focus our professional ministerial lives on providing care for victims, survivors, and those who love them. But if you are caring for people in any capacity and the Bible is part of your world, you need to develop the empathy, honest recognition, and critical curiosity that will be the start of a journey in providing trauma-informed care. Trauma-informed interpretation can be a safe and meaningful place to start.

Make no mistake: this is not a therapy textbook—though I would be very interested to hear if it is ever used as such one day. Instead, this is an invitation to reread some of our foundational stories of faith with new eyes to see what many of us have been missing and how we can be drawn deeper to the fullness of Scripture. In doing so, we will develop language and experiences to ask what stories might be behind the stories we are comfortable telling and hearing. Allowing ourselves as the body of Christ to get curious about hidden or overlooked stories is how God draws near to the brokenhearted and how we can partner in God's rescue of those who are crushed in spirit.

People of faith have used different methods over the centuries to grapple with scriptural texts. One source for delving deeper into the Hebrew Bible that Christians often miss is the rich trove of commentary found in the Jewish extrabiblical writings. I will make ample use of a genre of writing called midrash (literally, "from study"). Midrash is a technique of interpreting Scriptures by looking for connections, seeking to fill gaps, and drawing seeming contradictions into harmony. Midrash is a Jewish practice, ancient and modern, and was fairly widespread across Judea and the diaspora. Accordingly, midrash can be found in both Talmuds (Jerusalem and Babylonian) but also in independent works. Notably for this work, a collection of midrashim (the plural of *midrash*) focused on Genesis, Genesis Rabbah, began compilation around the fourth century CE and came into its final form centuries later. I will draw heavily from it.

It is important to note that Christians will have already encountered midrash in their New Testament readings. As just one of many examples, Paul appropriates a well-known midrash to point to Christ's presence. In Exodus 17, Moses strikes a rock to bring forth water in the desert for the thirsty Israelites. In Numbers 20, Moses again strikes a rock to bring forth potable water. Some modern biblical scholars see this repetition as evidence of merged narratives recording the same episode in different settings. However, Jewish readers noticed these two similar episodes of rocks giving water (and Israelites singing to a well to give water in Num 21:17–18) and reasoned that if a rock could give water miraculously, it could also roll along with the community on its own. Which is more likely—two water rocks or one that accompanied the tribes? Thus, the notion of a rock that accompanied the Israelites from Rephidim to Kadesh was born from careful study of two similar but separate events. In 1 Corinthians 10:4, Paul references in passing the rock that accompanied the Israelites in the wilderness, claiming that it was Christ with the people. An *accompanying* rock is not in the Bible, but it is in the Talmud (b. Taan. 9a) and midrashic collection on Numbers (Num. Rab. 1:1). Paul uses that midrash to understand better the work and presence of God. We seek to do the same.

One final note: this work is personal for me. I have been a Hebrew Bible scholar for decades. For almost as long, I have been a survivor of sexual assault. But I had no idea about the depth and intensity of the effects that the trauma continued to have on me until I started to receive trauma-informed care that took seriously the ways I had been hurt and the ways that my healing was incomplete, particularly as a cis-het male survivor.[3] This care involved asking lots of questions and telling lots of stories. A truly massive part of my healing journey has

---

3. By *cis-het*, I mean that my gender identity matches my sex assigned at birth, and I, as a man, am exclusively attracted to women.

been to feel "the family" in Genesis empathize with me through their stories. Jacob, Tamar, and Dinah knew what it was to be preyed upon and then to have their own hurt minimized, dismissed, or disregarded completely by those close to them, for whom the truth about the abuse was inconvenient or too painful to bear. Suddenly, people and characters I thought I knew my whole life opened their stories and shared their strength, guiding me in how I could survive and recover as they did. This is what God wanted for me and also wants for you.

"The Lord is near to the brokenhearted And saves those who are crushed in spirit" (Ps 34:18). The human lives in Genesis testify that God was close to them before, during, and after experiences of gendered trauma, and therefore God will be close to me and to all who suffer. God saves those who were crushed in spirit—repeatedly—and so God will save us too.

And that saving, like this book, is often a journey rather than a single shining moment. The book will proceed accordingly. Chapters 1–2 will focus on the experiences of Sarah and of Lot's daughters as they recover from sexual trauma inflected on them by their families. We will pay particular attention to the ways that Sarah's sexual assault in Egypt may have influenced her abusive treatment of her Egyptian servant, Hagar/HaGar. Similarly, Lot's willingness to subject his daughters to sexual assault in order to save himself and his male guests plays a foundational role in the rape and sexual coercion practiced by his daughters. The chapters close with discussions of healing from gender-based sexual trauma and breaking cycles of abuse.

Chapter 3 focuses on the neglect and abuse of Jacob, Leah, and Joseph by their families and those who were responsible for providing for them. Each of these three characters resists abuse by consciously performing their gender differently, creating a mask and a new self in the process. We will explore trauma's ability to destabilize a sense of self and Judith Butler's theory of gender performativity to reflect that healing cannot mean going back but rather must mean moving forward.

Chapter 4 considers the story of Dinah, as an isolated ethno-religious minority who is "taken" and "made low" by a prince of the land into which her family has moved. In a story in which Dinah does not speak, how can thoughtful interpreters resist the impulse to turn her into a ventriloquist dummy, putting their/our words in her mouth? Exploring Dinah's story serves as a reminder to hold space for victims of trauma and to actively work against secondary traumas of silencing, shaming, and decentering the victims themselves.

Chapter 5 is a brief departure from Genesis based on the rabbinic identification of Job's wife with Dinah of Genesis 34. How does Dinah's survival of sexual assault give her moral clarity to speak truthfully of God and support her husband through his traumatic experience, even while undergoing deep loss herself? This chapter seeks to undermine sexist and misogynist interpretations of Job's wife and instead to learn from her experience and wisdom.

Chapter 6 explores the story of Tamar as she was literally passed around in Judah's family and how she finally exerts control over her sexuality and reproductivity. The chapter explores the ways in which Tamar's body was used for pleasure, but when she accessed her own agency, she was convicted of a capital crime. It was only her own wisdom and cunning that prevented her murder and the deaths of her unborn children. The chapter explores the relationships between sexual abuse and legal, economic, and judicial power.

Chapter 7 delves into the story of Joseph. The rabbis have long suspected Joseph of performing gender queerly. How does a queer, foreign slave resist sexual assault and navigate mistreatment by the legal system in which he has a triple disadvantage? After Joseph is traumatized first by his family and then by his owner's spouse, he finds a pathway to resistance and freedom. But the chapter ends by returning to the theme of the first chapter—hurt people hurt people. Joseph's undealt-with pain leads him to fatal abuses of power.

The book ends with a plea for victims of trauma, and those who love them/us, to continue to engage in the work of healing and exploration of their/our own experiences.

1

LEARNING TO READ

Scripture: Genesis 12, 16, 20–21

TRAUMA IS NOT merely extreme hurt; rather, it is an injury so severe that it does not allow the body, mind, and soul to heal or find meaning without help. Irene Landsman points out, "Trauma and loss are experiences that push us to our limits. By definition, trauma overwhelms our usual abilities to cope and adjust, calling into question the basic assumptions that organize our experiences of ourselves, relationships, the world, and the human condition itself."[1] There is a finite amount of pain that humans can deal with, metaphorically metabolize, and clear from their systems. Trauma is different, and it becomes a sort of sticking point that we are unable to move past because it is a greater injury than our biological, emotional, mental, and spiritual systems are equipped to deal with. Without specific, professional help, and even sometimes then, trauma overwhelms human experience and changes human behavior.

A well-known adage in counseling circles reminds us that the seeds of abusive behavior are frequently found in past experiences of trauma or abuse: "Hurt people hurt people."[2] Resmaa Menakem theorizes in *My Grandmother's Hands* that all experienced pain and

---

1. Irene Smith Landsman, "Crisis of Meaning in Trauma and Loss," in *Loss of the Assumptive World: A Theory of Traumatic Loss*, ed. Jeffery Kauffman (New York: Brunner-Routledge, 2002), 13.

2. Kelly E. O'Connor et al., "'Hurt People Hurt People': Relations between Adverse Experiences and Patterns of Cyber and In-Person Aggression and Victimization among Urban Adolescents," *Aggressive Behavior* 47, no. 4 (July 2021): 483–92.

trauma will be acted on and passed on to other people.³ The choice that humans must make is whether they will pass along "clean pain," which is processed with integrity and faces fears of unknown journeys toward healing, or "dirty pain," when wounded parts of the human act out in fear. Passing along dirty pain only creates more pain, both for the original sufferer and for additional recipients of pain.

At the beginning of the patriarchal narratives of Genesis, two women, Sarah and HaGar, are traumatized victims of sexual assault. They respond differently to their abuse, acting in turn to pass on dirty or clean pain to those around them. This chapter does not seek to exonerate or condemn but to read with a close eye what happens when profound pain is passed on to others rather than recognized, addressed, and healed. Sarah's experience of traumatic and dehumanizing abuse in Egypt and Gerar will be essential for understanding her abusive treatment of HaGar.

A final note before proceeding: What follows has been written (and edited) by trauma survivors. But it may not be your time to read this yet. In the interest of working toward clean pain, please proceed carefully after considering what is the healthiest and most restorative path for you.

Names

I need to give a brief note on how I will use names, in this chapter especially but also in those that follow. When someone undergoes a major life or bodily transition of the sort that Abraham and Sarah face in and after Genesis 17, they frequently change names to mark their new bodily reality. The text of Genesis uses "Abram" and "Sarai" until their names change. But God insists that they will be called Abraham and Sarah, noting explicitly that Sarah will no longer be called Sarai

---

3. Resmaa Menakem, *My Grandmother's Hands: Racialized Trauma and the Pathway to Mending Our Hearts and Bodies* (Las Vegas: Central Recovery, 2017).

(Gen 17:15). I want to follow God and use the names that they come to be known by after they experienced embodied miracles that allowed them to be who God called them to be. Accordingly, I will not use deadnames.

HaGar's name is presented in the same verse in which she is introduced (Gen 16:1). HaGar's name is clearly important to the story, but it also is a point of confusion. Hagar (הָגָר) is possibly a loanword from another language rather than Hebrew. Nahum Sarna sees a connection with the Arabic *hagara*, as someone who travels and maybe a fugitive, referencing HaGar's flight in Genesis 15:6.[4] I think it may be better here to stay closer to the text and see HaGar's name as a sort of title used by Sarah: "the foreigner"/ha-Gar (*ha* would serve as the definite article to *gar* as "foreigner"). Since so much of the story of their interaction is seen through the lens of Sarah's attempts to use and control her, and the culmination of the story is HaGar's emancipation and reunification with her own people, I think it is most honoring of HaGar's experience in the household of Abraham to remember that she is HaGar—the foreigner, who ultimately leaves bondage and Canaan. I will capitalize the *G* in HaGar for this reason.

Growing Up under Terah

How do we understand Sarah as a person? Is she a giant of faith who left Ur and Haran, and everyone and everything she knew, to go with her husband to a strange land where they did not even speak the language? Is she a monster who forced her slave to bear a child for her, and then tried to condemn her slave and even her husband's child to death? Was she a repeated victim of what we would today call sex trafficking? Was she a mother simply trying to protect her son from men and boys in her family whom she knew to be dangerous? What drives Sarah and makes her tick? What are her motivations for going

---

4. Nahum Sarna, *Genesis*, JPS Torah Commentary (Philadelphia: Jewish Publication Society, 1989), 119.

with Abraham and staying with him? What does she want out of life? What is she scared of?

The biblical text does not describe Sarah nearly as extensively as Abraham or other male characters. The situations that Sarah goes through, however, and the difficulties she faces—and causes—are described in poignant detail. Sarah is unique among the matriarchs in that we have a relatively full picture of her life. We know where she was born: Ur. We know who her father (or at least male ancestor) was: Terah. We know her husband: Abraham. We know her journeys. And we know that she has agency, disagreeing with Abraham and giving him commands, even to do things he did not want to do. God tells Abraham, "Whatever Sarah tells you, listen to her" (Gen 21:12). How did Sarah come to wield such power and prerogative with her patriarch husband?

From the text we know that Sarah is part of Abraham's clan and is maybe even his sister. Sarah is introduced in Genesis 11:29: "Abram and Nahor took wives for themselves. The name of Abram's wife was Sarai, and the name of Nahor's wife was Milcah, the daughter of Haran, the father of Milcah and Iscah." Later Abraham will say, when caught being deceptive about his relationship to Sarah, that she is his sister, the daughter of his father but not of his mother (Gen 30:12). But is Abraham being fully truthful here? Relationships described as

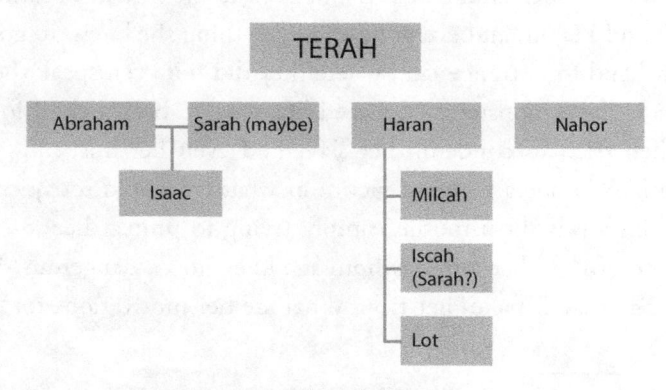

Figure 1.1 Terah family tree

"sister" and "daughter-in-law" could be flexible and indicate a close female relative but could also be literal. Modern scholars and ancient rabbis suggest that Sarah was probably Abraham's niece. That parallels the account in Genesis 11:29 above and seems to support that Nahor married his niece, Haran's daughter, and Abraham married their other niece. The rabbis identify Sarah with Iscah (b. Sanh. 69b). Iscah, meaning something like "watchful" or "observant," is an apt name for Sarah, who will have to watch out for dangerous situations from male relatives for the rest of her life.

Whether half-sister or niece, Sarah was a younger member of Abraham's household before marriage. She grew up around her relative Abraham, who was ten years her senior. At the ages of one hundred and ninety, this difference is inconsequential, but at twenty and ten or fifteen and five, the difference is much starker.

We know nothing about their engagement, marriage, or feelings for each other, unlike the profoundly loving relationship between their son Isaac and daughter-in-law Rebekah. What we do know is that Sarah was taken by men in her family when and where they wanted. Abraham "takes" Sarah (*laqah*) as a wife (Gen 11:29). This is the commonly used phrase for marriage, to be sure, and we should not see in Abraham something unusual. But the cultural notion of a woman as someone to be taken is significant. Additionally, Terah takes Sarah from Ur to Haran (11:31). Abraham takes Sarah (and his nephew Lot) from Haran to Canaan (12:5). Lot is mentioned as going with Abraham by his own agency in 12:4 before being taken. Sarah, however, continues to be taken.

The question of a woman consenting to being taken, either in marriage or on a journey, does not arise here (we will spend much time on the question when we get to Dinah). Sarah has a different experience from her daughter-in-law Rebekah (who is probably also her niece), who does choose to be married and to go on a journey to meet her betrothed. Sarah is a woman who is not asked what she wants. She is simply taken by her father and her husband.

Infertility and "Making Souls"

As Abraham, Sarah, and Lot are preparing to leave Haran, they assemble their belongings, including "all the acquisitions that they had acquired and *souls which they had made [nefesh asher asu]*" (Gen 12:5, my translation). The text is not clear about who was making souls, but a plural "they" has been making people who are taken to Canaan. The first thing that we learn about Sarah outside her relationship to Abraham is that she is infertile. Genesis 11:30 states: "Sarai was unable to conceive; she did not have a child." But how does one know who in the relationship is unable to have children? A few chapters later, we read, "Sarai, the wife of Abram, did not bear children *for him*" (16:1, my translation). As Sarah contemplates intervening in their later quest to have a child, is finding another sexual partner for Abraham a novel idea or a remembered practice? Sarah has not borne children "for him," but the text claims that someone else had.

Has Sarah already missed the boat on providing Abraham an heir even before they leave Haran? Abraham does not seem to think so. In Genesis 15, Abraham regards himself as childless while naming Eliezer of Damascus as his heir. Abraham and Sarah were never without servants, even before they set out from Haran. Eventually, their household grew to include hundreds of servants (14:14). Yet only Eliezer of Damascus is named (15:2), other than HaGar. Eliezer may very well have been one of the souls Abraham made with a servant from Damascus before receiving the call to leave Haran.

When God calls Abraham to leave Haran, the call comes to him explicitly, and the text says nothing about Sarah's role in the promise.

> *Now the LORD said to Abram,*
> *"Go from your country,*
> *And from your relatives*
> *And from your father's house,*
> *To the land which I will show you;*
> *And I will make you into a great nation,*

> *And I will bless you,*
> *And make your name great;*
> *And you shall be a blessing;*
> *And I will bless those who bless you,*
> *And the one who curses you I will curse.*
> *And in you all the families of the earth will be blessed."*
> *(Gen 12:1–3)*

After Abraham hears God's call to go to Haran, Lot is mentioned before Sarah and more often (12:4–5). Is Sarah even a part of the initial planning, or is she simply grouped with possessions and recently made souls that are taken on the journey?

Is anyone certain of Sarah's role in God's promise? I think the answer must be no. Does she have any part in what God has promised Abraham? Sarah herself is not sure. After all, Sarah suggests Abraham take HaGar as a wife to bear a child (16:3). After Ishmael is born to HaGar and Abraham, God tells Abraham that he will have a child through Sarah as well. Abraham's first response is to laughingly refuse and simply ask that Ishmael will live in God's sight (17:15–18). It is only at God's insistence that Sarah is explicitly made part of the divine promise.

Prior to Sarah having maidservants to give to her husband or receiving promised children, however, the first matriarch endures the first in a series of repeated traumatizing events that will shape her behavior and outlook for the rest of her life. Abraham's and Sarah's initial sojourn in the promised land is relatively short. As the result of a famine in the land, they make their way down to the perennially fertile land of Egypt.

What Happened in Egypt?

Like much of Southwest Asia did during times of food shortage, Abraham and Sarah turned to Egypt, with its predictable Nile floods and corresponding plentiful harvests. But on the way to Egypt, as they drew near to their destination, Abraham had something of an epiphany. Abraham suddenly came to know that Sarah, his wife, was beautiful. The Hebrew is explicit: "See now, I know that you are a beautiful woman" (Gen 12:11). Nothing has changed for Sarah. Instead, Abraham is seeing her in a new way.

The rabbis insist that Sarah is no ordinary beauty but is among the most beautiful women in history, like Rahab, Abigail, and Hadassah/Esther (b. Meg. 14a). Indeed, only Eve is manifestly more lovely than Sarah (b. B. Bat. 58a). Perhaps another implication of Sarah's other name, Iscah (remember, *Iscah* has connotations of "looking" or "watching"), was that all people wished to gaze (*sokhim*) at her splendor. Sarah's beauty was not a passing stage, either. Even in her ninetieth year, Sarah was said to be as comely as a bride at her wedding (Gen. Rab. 45:4).

So, how did Abraham, who was married to Sarah and grew up in the same clan as her, fail to know she was beautiful until they drew near to Egypt? The rabbis have a few ideas. First, it may be that Abraham was so used to Sarah's presence that he never understood how beautiful she was until they went on a long journey. As the days and weeks stacked on to one another, Abraham and those servants who accompanied them started to look increasingly haggard and weary from the road. In contrast, Sarah remained looking fresh, strong, rested, and vibrant (Gen. Rab. 40:4).

Another suggestion for why Abraham only suddenly realized that Sarah was beautiful rests on Abraham comparing Sarah to every other woman that he saw. As they passed through the land of Aram-Naharaim and then the land of Nahor, Sarah was manifestly more beautiful than everyone that Abraham saw. But these places were relative backwaters. When Abraham drew near to the bustling, cosmopolitan cities of Egypt, and he saw women from all over the world, he finally knew that his own wife was profoundly beautiful. This characterization of Abraham, as shamelessly looking at every other woman, evaluating them by physical beauty alone, comparing them to his own wife, and thinking about how the beauty of women might affect him, carries the narrative forward.

Abraham asks Sarah to tell the Egyptians that she is his sister rather than his wife because he supposes that the Egyptians will kill him and take her. Abraham projects his own patriarchal desire to have the most beautiful wife onto the Egyptians he is encountering for the first time. Abraham claims to Sarah that the Egyptians practice the violent masculinity that he himself has imagined and foisted on them. Abraham begs Sarah to make herself sexually available to protect him. Let us not mince words: Abraham renouncing exclusive marital claims to Sarah is *exactly* what this "sister" language is about. We know this because of the next couple of verses.

Predictably, the Egyptians take much less time than Abraham to see that Sarah is indeed incredibly beautiful (Gen 12:14). The servants of Pharoah praise her to their master, and Sarah is "taken into Pharoah's house" (Gen 12:15). The text is more explicit a few verses later, when Pharoah says that he took Sarah as his wife (Gen 12:19). Sarah becomes Pharoah's wife in all ways.

But what of Abraham during Sarah's time in Pharoah's house? He became rich for passing off his wife as his sister. The text says that Pharoah literally "did good" to Abraham "on her account" and gave him sheep, oxen, donkeys, male servants and female servants, and camels. Make no mistake: this was not a goodwill gift but rather a bride price paid to the family giving a young woman for marriage. Abraham sold his wife/niece/sister into marriage in a foreign land.

Sarah had only known her husband from her own clan, and suddenly she was in a large household, married to a man with presumably hundreds of other sexual partners, whose customs, practices, language, and bodies were all literally foreign to her. The man who brought her hundreds of miles away from her people and her home had sold her for animals and slaves. She was isolated and alone, unable to escape or make plans for herself. This is the definition of sex trafficking. The isolation, confusion, and dehumanization of being exchanged for great wealth by a man who was responsible for her could not be other than deeply traumatic. With whom could Sarah share her immense hurt, her feelings of betrayal, her confusion, or her hopelessness as she became part of Pharoah's harem, seemingly without potential for another life?

Or, and this is a distinct possibility, did Sarah enjoy Egyptian life? Did she enjoy living in a society that noticed her beauty right away rather than taking multiple years to see her? Did Pharoah's servants continue to praise her every day, as they had when they first saw her? Did Sarah appreciate that a man would give riches to keep her rather than sell her for riches? Was the initial emotional and sexual trauma of being repudiated and sold as a sexual partner compounded by being returned to the man who sold her in the first place?

As the plagues struck everyone in Pharoah's house, except for Sarah (Gen 12:17), her isolation, fear, and trauma only increased. The text does not describe how Pharoah came to the knowledge that Sarah was really Abraham's wife as well as his close family member. Later, when Abraham will again pass off Sarah as his sister and therefore sexually available, God will warn Abimelech of Gerar to free her and to let the couple go (Gen 20:3–7). God does not speak in Egypt in Genesis 12. Instead, Pharoah approaches Abraham with full knowledge of his deceit. Sarah has told her new husband everything.

Pharoah rightly explodes with anger and places the blame for the whole situation on Abraham. Instead of blaming Sarah, Pharoah asks: "Why did *you* [Abraham] say, 'She is my sister,' so that I took her for myself as a wife? Now then, here is your wife, take her and go!" (Gen 12:19). Pharoah is not just furious at being deceived. He wants Abraham to learn a lesson. *Behold your wife! She is not just your sister. Do not see her as your sister anymore. Behold Sarah as your wife. You have seen that Sarah is beautiful, as has all of Egypt. But you, Abraham, you saw her only as a means to stay safe and even get rich. Get out of here!* Pharoah instructs his men to send them away with all they have (Gen 12:20). Pharoah does not demand the return of the bride price paid to Abraham. He had, after all, acquired a wife, at least for a little while. That traumatic little while in Pharoah's harem had lasting repercussions for generations.

Sarah and HaGar: Abuse from Trauma

Sarah has been hurt. And Sarah is going to hurt others out of the deep pain she continued to experience. Richard Rohr teaches, "*If we do not transform our pain, we will most assuredly transmit it*—usually to those closest to us: our family, our neighbors, our co-workers, and, invariably, the most vulnerable, our children."[5] Sarah passes her hurt down to people even more vulnerable than her own children: namely, her slave, HaGar, and HaGar's son, Ishmael.

We must remember that in the ten years between the trauma in Egypt and the trauma that is about to happen in Canaan, Abraham's and Sarah's household has not remained static. Abraham and Sarah left Haran with a collection of "souls that they had made" (probably servants, but I want to leave that interpretive door open). Abraham acquired several more servants (and animals!) from giving Sarah to Pharoah. In the meantime, hundreds of people were being born in Abraham's house (Gen 14:14). We must not imagine that Sarah and Abraham are alone in a tent, though they may pass the heat of the day there while their servants are out working (18:1, 9). Instead, they have hundreds and probably thousands of servants and multiple generations together with them, probably mostly from Aramaean and Egyptian ancestry. These servants are having babies, and many of them will be Aramaean-Egyptian, like Ishmael. Sarah, as the matriarch of the whole camp, would have been confronted daily with the fertility of most other women in her household. Abraham and Sarah's lack of children, as their household expanded rapidly, would certainly have been a topic of embarrassment. This will become apparent later, when Sarah finally gives birth and her thoughts focus on a change in public

---

5. Richard Rohr, *A Spring within Us: A Book for Daily Meditations* (Sheridan, WY: CAC, 2016), 199, 120–21.

perception: "God has made laughter for me; *everyone* who hears will laugh with me. . . . *Who* would have said to Abraham that Sarah would nurse children? Yet I have given birth to a son in his old age" (21:6–7).

For ten long years, Sarah has felt social contempt for their inability to have children. Sarah locates the problem with herself rather than Abraham. So, Sarah starts to think of who a reproductive surrogate for her could be. Just as Abraham used Sarah's sexuality in Egypt and gained people and wealth, Sarah decides to use the sexuality of HaGar, one of her Egyptian servants, to gain children for herself. Sarah's choice is interesting here. Instead of suggesting one of their servants who journeyed with the household since the beginnings of their travels, or even one of the daughters who was born to the Aramean servants, Sarah delivers up to her husband an Egyptian sexual partner. Perhaps this should be understood as an unsubtle reminder for Abraham of Sarah's experience in Pharoah's house when *she* was taken as a wife. Sarah was traumatized, and she is willing to traumatize others in exactly the same way.

As horrific as someone else controlling a woman's sexuality is—and it is!—I must say a word about language and status. HaGar is not called in this passage a פִּילֶגֶשׁ/"concubine" or a זָנָה/"sex worker" or any similar term, despite some problematic translations. Sarah gave HaGar to Abraham *as his wife*. Perhaps HaGar's station would not have allowed her to be given as anything lower than a full wife. One tradition holds that HaGar was one of Pharoah's daughters by a different woman. Pharoah gave HaGar to Sarah as a reward (*agarekh*, a play on *Hagar*) to remember their time together. Pharoah reasoned that it was better for HaGar to be a servant in Sarah's house than a noblewoman in Egypt (Gen. Rab. 45:1). After marrying Abraham, however, HaGar was both a noblewoman and a servant. Sarah was now unable to do anything to HaGar without Abraham's permission (Gen 16:5–6). HaGar remained Sarah's slave, to be sure. But she was also one of Abraham's wives, and as such, Abraham's connection to HaGar superseded Sarah's.

We have no words in the text about HaGar's experience thus far. Thankfully, HaGar eventually speaks, and the text records at least something of her emotional and spiritual life. HaGar tells God that she is fleeing her (abusive) mistress and then praises the God whom she sees and who sees her (16:8–13). We do not know what HaGar thought or felt about Sarah, her mistress, giving HaGar as a wife to Abraham. That changes after HaGar realizes that she has become pregnant. As HaGar grew great with child, "Sarah grew smaller in her eyes" (16:4, my translation). Sarah's trauma response to seeing all the children being born in their household was to offer up sexuality to get what she wanted—not her own, but that of someone she controlled. Yet when HaGar realized that she was a wife of the master, and she, rather than Sarah, was giving Abraham a child, Sarah almost certainly shrank down to a shadow of herself.

At that moment it becomes clear to everyone involved that Sarah has been replaced. For the second time in a decade, Abraham received Egyptians' bodies by displacing Sarah from his bed as his wife. Remember, God said nothing about Sarah's role in making a great nation in Genesis 15. Abraham's first response to God telling him that Sarah would give birth to his heir is to laughingly refuse and ask that God would count HaGar's son as his heir (17:18). For all anyone knows, Sarah has been cast aside.

Sarah's pain at being demoted from a wife to a sister in Egypt has been transformed and magnified by having her slave—someone who she thought she could control and give away—replace her in bed, family, and status as the matriarch of the camp of thousands. Sarah's attempt to deal with her own trauma has instead multiplied trauma. Sarah is not finished, however, passing on "dirty pain."

Sarah complains to Abraham, HaGar's husband, against HaGar. Notably, Sarah does not lie or diminish the truth. Sarah tells Abraham what he already knows—Sarah has become small in HaGar's eyes. Abraham, never one to protect his wives from abuse, turns HaGar over to Sarah, knowing that his pregnant wife will suffer at the hands of his hurt and humiliated other wife. Sarah abuses HaGar so much that she self-emancipates and risks death outside the camp.

Even after HaGar returns to the camp at God's direction and gives birth to her son, Ishmael, Sarah continues to act out of hurt and trauma. Sarah has nothing to do with Ishmael after he is born. Crucially, Abraham names the boy, rather than Sarah (16:15), which is counter to reproductive surrogacy traditions elsewhere (30:1–24). The repetition of names in the verses insists on HaGar's role and Sarah's diminution: "So HaGar bore a son to Abraham; and Abraham named his son, to whom HaGar gave birth, Ishmael. Abraham was eighty-six years old when HaGar bore Ishmael to him" (16:15–16). There is no room for Sarah here, only HaGar.

Ultimately, Sarah will respond to interactions between Ishmael and her own future son, Isaac, by permanently banishing HaGar and Ishmael. Thankfully, with a miraculous provision of water, HaGar and Ishmael seem to thrive after they escape Sarah's trauma factory. HaGar returns to Egypt, her home, as a free woman, to acquire a wife for her own son. The deep trauma Sarah inflicted on HaGar by forcibly attempting to use her as a reproductive surrogate seems to have been prevented from becoming a generational wound, at least on this side of the family tree. Ishmael becomes a wild, undomesticated survivor who will be a slave to no one (16:12). However, Sarah's trauma is far from over.

Revisiting Trauma: Gerar

The public repudiation of Sarah as Abraham's wife is not a one-time event. As the nomadic household traveled, Sarah seems to have grown accustomed to Abraham renouncing marital union, at least temporarily. Later, Abraham will tell Abimelech that their portrayal of Sarah as available for marriage was their practice *everywhere* they went (Gen 20:13). Imagine Sarah's humiliation, hurt, and betrayal as her husband said that she was his relative rather than his wife and offered her to the household of every ruler they encountered.

Unsurprisingly, then, as Abraham and Sarah entered Gerar, Abraham once again apparently told anyone who would listen, "She is my sister." When word got around to King Abimelech, he "took" Sarah. Notably missing here is "as a wife." In fact, the text is insistent that nothing happened between Sarah and Abimelech. The king did not come near Sarah (20:4), and God prevented Abimelech from touching her (20:6). Abimelech returned Sarah to Abraham and gave gifts to Abraham after finding out that Sarah was already married as an incentive to settle anywhere in the land, away from Abimelech's household.

Before their departure, however, Abimelech also makes a gift of one thousand pieces of silver. Abimelech speaks to Sarah directly and tells her that he made the gift to her brother for the "shutting of eyes" against her, so that before everyone Sarah will be *nokakhat*. But what does that mean? Does a payment after a supposed sexual liaison not confirm suspicions rather than help silence them? The meanings of *nokakhat* can include something like "exonerated/vindicated" but also "reproved/rebuked." Abimelech wants the matter (and eyes on the matter) to be closed. But does he rebuke Sarah for her participation in the repeated deception, or does he give Abraham one thousand pieces of silver as a testimony that he did not touch Sarah?

A clue can be found in what happened to all the women of Abimelech's household. Unlike all the members of Pharoah's house who were struck by plagues, only the women of Abimelech's household suffered any deleterious effects. They were unable to conceive while Sarah resided among them. For the household to make that determination, Sarah's stay in Abimelech's household must have been at least a few months. After Abraham receives the silver, he prays for Abimelech (to prevent death), and for Abimelech's wife and all his female servants, so that they can conceive children again. It seems that the payment of silver must be some sort of public gift testifying that Abimelech did not have sexual relations with Sarah. She is publicly exonerated of having sex with someone other than her true husband (who publicly disclaimed that role).

The chapter closes with an example of God providing for Sarah. The Lord had completely closed all the wombs of Abimelech's household for Sarah (Gen 20:18). After years of traveling in a massive household that seemingly increased by the day, and being passed off as a sister rather than the wife that she truly was, God granted Sarah a few months away from her deceiving husband, her fecund Egyptian co-wife, and all the women giving birth in her own household. Sarah had been given away, once again, but no one touched her. God granted her protection and, one hopes, peace. But God will take yet more drastic steps to provide at least a measure of healing for Sarah.

God Offers Healing for Sarah

At several times throughout the sad narrative of Sarah's repeated traumatization, and Sarah's callous, traumatic treatment of HaGar in exactly the same ways that she had been abused herself, God sticks up for Sarah, especially to the man who mistreated her. After Abraham asks for the covenant to go through HaGar's son, God insists that Sarah will have a child, and he will be Abraham's main heir. God says, "No, but your wife Sarah will bear you a son, and you shall name him Isaac; and I will establish My covenant with him as an everlasting covenant for his descendants after him" (Gen 17:19). God will also bless Ishmael, multiplying him exceedingly and bringing forth twelve princes from him who will become a great nation, mirroring promises made to Isaac. Remembering Sarah does not mean forgetting HaGar, not for God, and not for us, either. bell hooks insists on holding simultaneously the humanity and the responsibility of perpetrators to provide restitution to those whom they have hurt.[6] God seeks to do both, and we must as well.

---

6. Maya Angelou, bell hooks, and Melvin McLeod, "'There's No Place to Go but Up'—Bell Hooks and Maya Angelou in Conversation," Lion's Roar, January 1, 1998, https://www.lionsroar.com/theres-no-place-to-go-but-up/.

At the trees of Mamre, God, with angels, appears to Abraham and announces again that Sarah will have a son. Just as Abraham laughed in the previous chapter, Sarah laughs to herself at the idea now, saying, "After I have become old, am I to have pleasure, my lord being old also?" (Gen 18:12). When questioned why she laughed, Sarah denies it, but the Holy Visitors insist that she did. Still, God offers no reproof for Sarah's laughing and lying, and imposes no punishment. Should Sarah, whom God stuck up for and saved out of the house of Pharoah, Abimelech, and who knows how many others in between, have known better than Abraham when (not) to laugh when potential pregnancies were discussed? I would argue that, if anything, Sarah can be forgiven more readily for "knowing" that she would never be able to conceive. If she had not conceived decades earlier, after Pharaoh took her as wife, Sarah may truly have "known" that she could not become pregnant. At any rate, the text seems to indicate that Abraham had stopped giving Sarah pleasure, feigning impotence from old age while still being able to remarry and father children after Sarah's death (25:1–4).

Into this sad situation of continual betrayal and then neglect, the text says that God was gracious to Sarah and did for Sarah as promised (21:1). Sarah's joy at finally having a child of her own, of having proof that she was Abraham's wife and not just his sharable sister, is overwhelming. Sarah exultantly cries out, "Who would have said to Abraham that Sarah would nurse children? Yet I have given birth to a son in his old age" (Gen 21:7).

Sarah's exclamation provokes a question: Is Sarah nursing *a child*, or is Sarah nursing *children*? Just as Sarah's shame and betrayal at being passed off as a sister was on full public display for her whole household and all the residents of the towns and cities they visited, so was her exoneration. A lovely Talmudic midrash proclaims that some doubted that Abraham and Sarah ever had a child of their own, instead adopting an orphan found in the marketplace of one of the cities. In order to prove that Sarah had a child, she used to nurse the children of all of her servants, as well as those of the various kings and princes who took her into their households, along with her own son, Isaac (b. B. Meṣ. 87a). After all her trauma, and even despite passing trauma on to HaGar, God miraculously provided a witness that Sarah had an heir who was all hers and a husband who was not just a brother.

Conclusion: Breaking Cycles of Abuse and Trauma

There is no avoiding the sadness and disappointment in these traumatic stories. As soon as God starts to interact with humans in the patriarchal narratives, those humans subject others to gender-coded abuse and sexual trauma. But this evil is not the end of these stories. God intervenes. God provides freedom for HaGar and Ishmael. HaGar gets for her son an Egyptian wife from her own people. Ishmael will be free and unconquerable all the days of his life as God keeps the divine promise to make Ishmael into a great and powerful nation.

After years of waiting, Sarah will finally have a son from her husband, Abraham. Isaac is a great joy for many reasons, not the least of which is that he is proof to everyone that Sarah is not an unmarried sister. She is Abraham's wife and the mother of his son. Isaac means that Abraham can never lie about Sarah's position in the family or pass her off to other men.

Sarah and HaGar both suffered grievously as their sexuality was controlled by others. However, they both did their best to seize control of their own narratives and provide healing experiences for themselves and for their children. Sarah's and HaGar's attempts to spare their children from pain and sexual abuse are not repeated, however, elsewhere in the Genesis text. Lot and his daughters provide counterexamples of reciprocal traumatizing behavior.

Implications for Ministry

We have all seen it in ministry: the pillar of the congregation who is both a foundation of the community and the emotional wrecking ball who undermines change and growth because of their own issues. Matriarchs and patriarchs in our communities are no more (and no less) flawed than Abraham and Sarah. The trauma that Abraham inflicted on Sarah was a poisonous well that Sarah poured out to HaGar and to all the children of Abraham, affecting subsequent generations. How do we filter the water of life in our own congregations to stop the spread of emotional sickness?

The cure seems to be seeing selves and others rightly. Pharoah commanded Abraham to see Sarah as his wife and therefore to see himself as her husband, rather than as her pimp. Abimelech paid a steep sum to Abraham so that the eyes of all those who saw Sarah as Abraham's property or as a rentable commodity would be closed forever to such a vision. HaGar testified that God saw her—not Abraham's disposable wife, not Sarah's servant, but HaGar herself. Finally, Sarah saw herself as she always dreamed—a full, whole human, capable of reproductive creativity on her own. Re-encountering whole selves after trauma is essential not just for healing but to prevent a cascade of abuse and retraumatization.

So, what gift is Sarah giving us? Sarah insists that we see the humanity of the callous, dismissive, racist, often older folks who are difficult to love on their best days. It was Sarah's dehumanization by her husband that set the context for the dehumanization she practiced against HaGar and Ishmael. The solution to dehumanizing behavior is not more of it but insistence of seeing whole human selves in the other. Sarah's heart was healed when her relationship with herself was healed.

The practice of ministering to difficult people cannot just be waiting for them to die, as I hear too often. No healing comes from that, and another injured human (is there any other kind?) will simply rise to take their place. Instead, we must have the Sarahs of the world tell their stories, for themselves and for the communities. Who hurt you? What did that do to your heart/soul/self? How have you spread that hurt? What would healing look like? Trauma festers as it obliterates self and causes shame and hiding. The antidote is to bring stories of pain and hurt into the light, as difficult as that process always is. The gift of Sarah's and HaGar's stories is to insist that the messy, painful, awful, and shameful are an inescapable part of the story we need to tell in order to heal and be whole.

2

GENDER BIAS AND OTHER PROBLEMS

Scripture: Genesis 19

They also said, "This one came in as a foreigner, and already he is acting like a judge; now we will treat you worse than them!"

—Genesis 19:9

BUILDING ON THE previous chapter's depiction of Sarah as both victim of Abraham and perpetrator of traumatic abuse against HaGar, this chapter analyzes the story of Lot and his daughters to help reveal biases in thinking about gender and trauma. Lot's willingness to subject his daughters to sexual assault to save himself and his male guests frames the later rape and sexual coercion practiced by his daughter(s) against him. As above with Sarah, HaGar, Abraham, and their children, Lot and his family's shared—but profoundly unequal—experiences of abuse shape the surviving family members' treatment of each other.

In discussing Lot and his daughters, much remains unsaid in the text. I would like clearer expressions of agency or disinterest surrounding sexual activity. But terse descriptions that leave more questions than answers are hardly surprising. Much of the experience of trauma consists of words being insufficient to describe or expound the intensity of suffering. Elizabeth Boase cautions the reader of traumatic stories, "The notion of a failure of language is central: trauma in its essence defies representation in normal discursive language. The presence of trauma, however, must be witnessed in imaginative literature, in figurative language."[1] In the Bible, as in everyday conversation, there is seldom a flashing red sign that says, "Depiction of trauma ahead: caution!" Instead we must look to language that gets at but does not quite capture the indescribable experience of trauma.

One of the most noticeable silences in Genesis 19 is that Lot's wife and two daughters are unnamed. For unnamed characters such as Lot's daughters, I try to use names that are developed in secondary literature or commentary. Unnamed women known only by their relationship to a man are a symptom of toxic patriarchy in both Bible times and our own; identification of a whole human being by simple attachment to a man is insufficient. In her womanist midrash, Wil Gafney names Lot's daughters Zeqenah ("Elder-Woman") and Qetenah ("Younger-Woman"). I will follow Rev. Dr. Gafney's naming convention with gratitude.

Lot and His Daughters: Threats and Assault

The sexual assaults that receive the most attention in the story of Sodom are those threatened against the angelic visitors (Gen 19:5) and then against Lot himself (19:9). Every time this passage is discussed, we must remind ourselves that the people of Sodom are trying to abuse foreigners ("the men who came to you," 19:5; "this one came in as a foreigner," 19:9). Jude 1:7 notes that the men of Sodom went after "other," ἑτέρας, flesh. The point is that Sodom and the cities of the plain brutally subverted norms of hospitality and caring for the needy (Ezek 16:49–50) and were condemned for their violence toward visitors, not for homosexuality.

Two sets of victims are often overlooked in discussions of the sexual assault in Sodom. First, Lot offered his two virgin daughters who still lived with him to the crowd insistent on raping foreigners (19:8).

---

1. Elizabeth Boase, "Fragmented Voices: Collective Identity and Traumatization in Lamentations," in *Bible Through the Lens of Trauma*, ed. Elizabeth Boase and Christopher G. Frechette (Atlanta: SBL Press, 2016), 52.

Second, Lot's daughters intentionally got Lot drunk and had sexual relations with their father, seemingly unbeknownst to him. These traumatic sexual assaults are the foci of the rest of this chapter. Lot's exposing of his daughters to sexual violence causes trauma and fear that will provide a context for his own abuse at the hands of those he exposed to abuse. Hurt people continue to hurt people.

We must remember trauma's power to undermine healthy, normal understandings of self and the world as well as normal understandings of how relationships work. Boase reminds the reader that trauma is "disruptive of notions of self and shatters assumptions that the world is good or safe; that justice is inevitable, or even possible; that life can be predictable; that the self has any control or worth; or that there can be a good or responsible divine power that allows trauma to happen."[2] Judith Lewis Herman insists, "Traumatized people suffer damage to the basic structures of the self. They lose their trust in themselves, in other people, and in God. Their self-esteem is assaulted by experiences of humiliation, guilt, and helplessness. . . . The identity they have formed prior to the trauma is irrevocably destroyed."[3] For victims of trauma to behave in unexpected, surprising, even injurious ways that compound trauma for themselves and those close to them is not unusual.

The core of each of the following stories of trauma and its aftermath is that humans experience some emotional, moral, or sexual injury that is simply too much to shrug off and bear but rather leads to a breakdown. The experience of trauma is frequently an inflection point in the lives of people, and especially of those described in the biblical text. After an isolating experience that defies simple communication or meaning making, how does one move on?

---

2. Boase, "Fragmented Voices," 51.

3. Judith Lewis Herman, *Trauma and Recovery: The Aftermath of Violence—From Domestic Abuse to Political Terror* (New York: Basic Books, 2015), 56.

"Since When Do Daughters Rape Their Fathers?" Minority Reports of Abuse

In her incisive womanist rereading of the story of Lot's daughters, Gafney asserts that not only did Lot happily participate in his own daughters' performatively nonconsensual sex with him, but he engineered the situation to make it seem like they were manipulating him when the opposite was true.[4] Gafney asks rhetorically, "Since when do daughters rape their fathers?" assuming that such a thing is unimaginable in the real world.

Indeed, according to available statistics, in the United States approximately 91 percent of victims of rape and/or sexual assault identify as female, and only approximately 9 percent identify as male. Fully 99 percent of perpetrators identity as male. And yet, my assailant was part of that 1 percent, and I am part of the 9 percent. However, my assailant and I were of the same age; when age differences become a factor, the issue becomes more complex. Gafney is right to insist that rape of an older man by a younger woman is, statistically, incredibly unlikely. A woman is profoundly less prone to rape a man, let alone her father.

My own commitment in life and in biblical exegesis, however, is to default toward believing survivors—whoever they are—and in disputed cases to investigate the matter thoroughly. We have in the story of Lot and his daughters at least three conflicting witnesses. First, the text details how two women collaborated intentionally and repeatedly to use intoxicants to have sex with an impaired man. Second, as I have noted, real-world data attest that women raping men is statistically unlikely, and young women raping older men is more unlikely yet. But third, I want to bring an antipatriarchal voice to witness this story as well.

---

4. Wil Gafney, "Lot Sexually Manipulates His Two Daughters," The Torah.com, 2021, https://www.thetorah.com/article/lot-sexually-manipulates-his-two-daughters.

Cisgender women are not the only folks harmed by patriarchy. Queer folks are profoundly affected, and multiply marginalized folks, unsurprisingly, are affected in multiple ways. Men who are complicit in upholding, defending, and expanding patriarchal systems, however, are often also victims of unjust systems that they support. So, as we will discuss in later chapters addressing how patriarchy led to frequently overlooked sexual violence against Jacob and Joseph, we must note that the sexual violence alleged to have been committed against Lot is frequently downplayed, minimized, explained away, or somehow made his fault. Thinking that a man cannot be raped by women is the height of (cisgender-heterosexual) patriarchal thinking: men do sex to others, women have sex done to them. A robust feminist framework will affirm that patriarchy is bad for everyone and will seek liberation *for everyone.* If we do not want to discount female survivors of sexual violence or look for ways that the reported assault might have been their fault, we should extend that same sensibility to *all* those who report traumatizing violence.

In this case of reported sexual violence, when experience, expectations, and reports differ, we must thoroughly investigate. Deuteronomy 19:16–19 provides a short but pointed instruction for resolving the case of conflicting witnesses when (at least) one is lying to obfuscate the truth: the judges should דָּרְשׁוּ הֵיטֵב (*dareshu hetev*; Deut 19:18). Frequently, this is translated as "investigate thoroughly," and that makes a lot of sense. *Darash* has connotations of inquiring or even studying and comes from a root that circles around the idea of seeking or repeatedly treading toward something. The idea is that this investigation of confounding witnesses would be methodical. An investigation by those who wish to resolve the issue must address the facts, witnesses, and place of dispute. The issue cannot be sorted out remotely but must be investigated like detectives in a movie or TV crime show, by people standing in the middle of the witnesses, facts, and scenes—not like a true-crime podcast host pontificating from a distance on what might have happened (though I love true crime!).

For the story of Lot and his daughters, a close reading of the text is one of the best investigations we can muster. At the same time, we must be intentional in listening both to the disquieting statistical anomaly of younger women raping an older man and to our feminist commitment to believe survivors. We will dwell in the scene and tread in the paths of those involved.

Foreshadowing

The events in the cave outside Zoar are the culmination of a lot of vileness up to that point. The stories of abuse, neglect, and exposure to harm, however, start much earlier. The text contrasts Lot with the men of Sodom mainly in how they treat foreign guests. The townsmen want to humiliate the visitors by raping them, to show the guests how profoundly unwelcome they are. Lot, a photonegative to the men of Sodom, is willing to let his own unmarried daughters be sexually assaulted and/or raped at the whim of the men of Sodom in order to protect the sojourners who have come under his protection. I would argue that both positions are absolutely horrible. The traumatizing horror of Lot's daughters hearing their own father offer them up as sacrificial replacement targets for sexual violence is matched only by the certainty that there are still parents in this world who willingly offer up their own children for sexual exploitation. Thankfully, in the case of Lot's household, the angelic visitors are there to prevent Lot from rewarding violence with more opportunities to inflict violence.

The angels strike all the men of Sodom blind and tell Lot to go and gather whomever else he has in the city. Imagine Lot sheepishly dodging and avoiding the scores of blind men grasping at anything that might help them in their blindness. Lot apparently makes several stops. He stops at the homes of at least a few sons-in-law who had married his other daughters, and possibly a few sons (19:12–13). The sons-in-law refuse his invitation to flee and keep their wives, Lot's married daughters, with them, so Lot flees with only his "two daughters *who are here*" (19:15). The text does not say whether Lot tried to convince his sons to leave too, or whether perhaps Lot recognized them in the violent mob outside his house. In any case, Lot's family—Lot, his wife, two unmarried daughters, married daughters and sons-in-law, and sons—seems to have been much larger than the ten righteous people whom Abraham was hoping would save the city (18:32). Alas, it was not to be.

Lot's sons-in-law make a telling observation about Lot. He seems to them כִּמְצַחֵק ("as one who mocks/engages in sex play"; 19:14). Several times in Genesis, this verb is used to signify various actions. When Abraham and Sarah hear that they will have a child together, they both "laugh." After Isaac is born, Sarah observes Ishmael "laughing" (21:9). But does this mean he is mocking Isaac, molesting someone, or just having a good time? Years later, Abimelech recognizes that Isaac and Rebekah are not brother and sister but husband and wife because he sees them "laughing" (26:8). Finally, Potiphar's wife accuses Potiphar of bringing Joseph to their household to "laugh" at her (39:14, 17). At least the last two, and possibly the last three, examples are describing some sort of sexual play. So when Lot's sons-in-law think of him as one who מְצַחֵק, it could be that he is a joker, but more likely they think he has inclined himself to the habits of the town. That is, Lot also may lust after foreign flesh. In wanting them to leave town with him, Lot's sons-in-law assume that Lot may go out of town and engage in transgressive sexual activities—which is exactly what happens, as it turns out, but not in the way that the sons-in-law imagine.

The text offers subtle hints that Lot has been accommodating himself to the ways of the men of Sodom. Each time the Genesis narrative reencounters Lot, he edges toward Sodom. After first claiming the land on the Jordan plain, Lot first sets up his tent *near* Sodom (13:12). By 14:12, Lot is living *in* Sodom. In 19:1, Lot is sitting *in the city gate*, having become one of the ruling men of Sodom. As a foreigner who gradually came to reside and then rule in Sodom, Lot must have had to acculturate dramatically. His sons-in-law, men of Sodom who did not join "both young and old, all the people from every quarter" (19:4), must have regarded their father-in-law as something of a dangerous disappointment, a man who rose to power by compromise with brutal xenophobia and bigotry rather than seeking to overthrow that violence. Sadly and ironically, the sons-in-law, in seeking to stay safe from Lot's games, whatever they may have been, condemn themselves and their families to die with the rest of Sodom. Lot has to abandon all but a few members of his family and flee.

Escape in Two Movements: Fear or Calculation?

Lot is slow to flee, even with the angelic visitors' insistence that leaving Sodom is a matter of life or death. The angels have to literally push Lot out of town. As he is leaving, they tell him to leave the entire area and flee to the mountains. Lot feels that he cannot make the journey to the mountains without the disaster overtaking him. Instead, he points out a town that is so small that its very name is "small" (Zoar). Surely such a small town can be spared and be a safe harbor where Lot and a few members of his family can stay as the disaster passes by. The angels agree to spare the tiny town for Lot's sake and not to start the punishment of the other cities of the plain until Lot and his family arrive (19:19–22).

Apparently, Lot, his wife, and two daughters flee in the wee hours of the morning and arrive at Zoar just at sunrise. At *exactly* that moment, fire and brimstone rain down on the cities of the plain because of their unjust abuse of foreigners. Lot (and apparently his daughters) are within the boundaries of Zoar and are accordingly safe. However, Lot's wife—who is behind him—turns and looks at the city of Sodom, no doubt thinking of her other children and grandchildren being incinerated. Because she is still outside the boundary of Zoar, behind rather than in front of Lot, she is turned to a pillar of salt. The connection with salt structures in the Dead Sea area is well known. I wonder, though, whether Lot's wife was turned into a physical manifestation of a mother suffering for her children. Her salty tears at the death of her children and the embodied memory of cradling her children within her own self—amniotic fluid and ocean water have the same quantity of salt—solidify in an instant, turning her into a monument to maternal loss and suffering at the death of children.

Frequently, we imagine that Lot's wife was turned to salt because she looked at the cities being destroyed. The next verses, however, indicate that this was probably not the cause. Abraham wakes up early and intentionally goes out to a place that affords an excellent view of Sodom and the other cities (vv. 27–28). Abraham is not turned to salt for viewing the destruction, and neither was Lot's wife; instead, she was simply not in the safety of Zoar, unable to force herself into safety when several of her children were not safe.

Lot, too, is affected by what he saw. As Zoar is only a tiny island of safety in a sea of destruction, Lot becomes afraid to stay there. How does one make a life when everything around is utter wasteland? So Lot takes his daughters up to the mountains, following the original instructions of the angels. They stay in a cave and wonder what is next.

What fear motivated the second movement toward safety? Was Lot afraid that the wickedness of tiny Zoar would provoke God's wrath? Did Lot not trust himself not to repeat his pattern of acculturating, in this case toward the practices of Zoar? After all, without his intervention Zoar would have been destroyed with the other cities. Or was Lot looking to isolate his daughters and feared there were still too many witnesses in the small hamlet?

The text describes a shaken Lot, so terrified of the coming destruction of Sodom that he is too paralyzed with fear to even take self-protective action. The angelic guests had to push him out of the town that he knew was about to be destroyed. Later, Lot is still afraid even while in a small village that survived the surrounding destruction. Lot flees from safety, reentering the danger zone that just killed his wife. Lot's dangerous paralysis and then reentry into dangerous ground sounds less like conniving to isolate his daughters and more like the trauma response of someone who has faced mob attack, destruction of home and property, and, most poignantly, the annihilation of several family members all in the last twenty-four hours. The text says that Lot left Zoar because of fear, but it would be fair to read that as abject terror after the destabilizing and traumatizing events of the preceding day.

Older and Younger

In the cave, Lot and his daughters must have felt absolute shock and numbness as events caught up with them and the adrenaline that carried them through the previous night and day crashed. Their siblings/children are dead. Their wife/mother is a salt pillar. Was Zoar consumed immediately after they left? The daughters seem to think that there was no one left in the world, even the tiny village of Zoar, whom they could marry. It would be fair to assume that no one in the cave was in a healthy emotional state.

It is not clear how long Lot and his daughters (again, I will use Zeqenah for the elder and Qetenah for the younger) reside in the cave before the daughters have a conversation about what to do with their father. The text is specific about how the idea to intoxicate and rape Lot is not mutually conceived between the two daughters. Instead, Zeqenah speaks directly to Qetenah, telling her that (1) their father is old and (2) there is not a man in the land (ארץ without the definite article should probably just be "land" here, rather than "earth"), according to the customs of the whole world (כל הארץ should probably be "all the earth" here; Gen 19:31). Did Zeqenah truly believe there were not any men left in the world, or just in the land? If Zoar was incinerated after they left, depending on the location of the cave in the mountains, the trio might only have seen smoldering waste and truly believed that they were the last humans on earth.

Therefore, Zeqenah hatches a plan to preserve the human race. The survival of the species, however, is not Zeqenah's only stated goal. Instead, Zeqenah appeals to her sister to preserve the seed of their father, not just have children (וּנְחַיֶּה מֵאָבִינוּ זָרַע, *unehayyeh meavinu zara*). Zeqenah is specifically talking about Lot's "seed" that she is trying to preserve in the earth. Not just any man will do for Zeqenah, even if there are others around. She is specifically speaking about taking power over Lot's body by means of intoxicating substances to at least nominally preserve his bloodline. Qetenah goes along with the plan the first night, cooperating in getting Lot just drunk enough to later not remember what happened but not so drunk that he cannot be coaxed into nonconsensual sex.

After that first night, when Qetenah does not seem to touch her father, Zeqenah tells her little sister what she did the previous night. She tells Qetenah that she should also rape their semiconscious father. Qetenah apparently agrees (Qetenah does not speak in the narrative, except to name her son) and has sex with her father.

The two accounts are *almost* identical, except for a few details. The older daughter twice convinces the younger daughter to go along with the plan. But what the two young women do and what Lot does differ slightly in the two episodes. The text says that Zeqenah "went in" and slept with her father (v. 33). In simplest terms, Zeqenah probably went into whatever part of the cave Lot was in. But the text leaves open her participation in the frequent double entendre of "going in" to a sexual partner (see Gen 29:23, 30). Qetenah does not "go in" but rather has to "go up," presumably as a person smaller than her father, to climb up on her naked and intoxicated father. This, of course, brings up a lot of questions about grooming and whether a minor who cannot consent can truly be thought of as a perpetrator after being groomed by her older sister.

If these verbs are describing sexual movements (and that "if" is doing a lot of work), Zeqenah, by "going in" to her father, is anally penetrating him in a revenge rape for all she suffered from him. Lot offered Zeqenah and Qetenah to a violent mob rather than protecting them. Lot acculturated enough to the detestable violence of Sodom that his own sons-in-law and other daughters were afraid that he would molest them. They stayed in the city rather than believing Lot's warnings, to their doom. And Lot did not even ensure that his wife, Zeqenah's and Qetenah's mother, was in a place of safety when the destruction came. Zeqenah has been terribly hurt and traumatized by her father in the last several days, and who knows for how long before that? At last, she gets some measure of revenge, by doing to him what Lot sought to let the crowds do to her and her little sister (Tanhuma, Vayera 12). Perhaps Zeqenah sought to give her little sister the opportunity to also take revenge rape, but Qetenah simply could not bring herself to do it. Instead, Qetenah seems to have been another victim of Zeqenah's quest for revenge, as, again, hurt people hurt people.

What Did Lot Know, and When Did He Know It?

We must ask, though, especially if Zeqenah committed not just non-consensual rape but violent, penetrative revenge rape, did Lot really not know anything? At first glance, the text seems to indicate that both evenings, Lot knew neither when his daughters lay down nor when they got up. However, an almost microscopic differences in verses 33 and 35 gives a hint that there might be more at play here.

Rabbinic interpretation of what happened in the cave hinges on the dot above וּבְקוּמָהּ (*ovequmah,* "and when she got up"). This scribal dot over the *vav* in verse 33 indicates that a scribe wanted a change but did not want to alter the manuscript tradition—probably advocating for a removal of the *vav,* as is the spelling in verse 35. However, some rabbis interpreted it to advocate for the removal of the whole word—Lot did not know when his oldest daughter *lay down,* but *he did know when she got up* (Gen. Rab. 51:8–9). Probably the pain of being anally raped by Zeqenah shocked him out of his semiconsciousness. According to this interpretation, Lot then willingly got drunk, or pretended to be drunk, to see what his daughters would do on the second night. Some rabbis apply Proverbs 18:1, "He who separates himself seeks desire" (my translation), to Lot, arguing that by leaving

Zoar to go to the mountains with his daughters, Lot was showing that he desired to rape his own daughters as he had offered to let the crowds do in Sodom.

However, a scribal dot to mark a different spelling of the same word two verses apart that would not have appeared in the early manuscript traditions seems like more of an opportunity to insert hyper-patriarchal doubt that men *can* be raped, rather than a compelling case that would undermine the narrative that the daughters got their father drunk so that they could have sex with him without his knowing when they lay down or got up. At least the understanding that Zeqenah "went in" to Lot as revenge rape is supported by the words in the textual tradition.

The Bible is a Rorschach test of sorts, and we can see whatever we bring to it. The text insists that Lot was raped. My commitment is to believe the survivors and investigate the reports. As closely as we can read the text, Zeqenah raped Lot. There is some doubt about whether Lot allowed himself to be intoxicated the next night, suspecting what would happen. But the reading that the older daughter sought control and revenge on Lot's sexuality, as hers had been so callously offered to the mob, seems the most straightforward—though, of course, this reading will seem unreasonable to those who do not believe that a woman can rape a man.

Whatever else happened, if the daughters deliberately intoxicated their father, the sex that followed was nonconsensual, as the text insists, and the rape of Lot in the cave is a story of perpetrators and at least one survivor. Zeqenah repeatedly pressuring her younger sister to get their father drunk and then have sex with him makes Zeqenah doubly a predator, and Qetenah another victim, even as Zeqenah pressured her to victimize their father.

As monstrous as these acts were, however, they were not committed in a vacuum. Lot horribly mistreated his daughters and willingly subjected them to sexual harm. And yet, no one, not even perpetrators themselves, deserves sexual violence in retribution. Zeqenah, in particular, passes along "dirty pain" and furthers the cycle of abuse, running counter to the normal generational flow. Even so, Moab and Ammon, the sons of Zeqenah and Qetenah, respectively, will be recognized as full-fledged family members of the Israelites and covenant partners with God (Deut 2:18–19, 37).

Conclusion

In these horrific stories of trauma and response, creating a new self is the only possibility for healthy practices of moving on for the survivors. As Tod Linafelt helpfully observes, "Survival does not prolong a life that is already dead; it initiates, in the death of what was there, the miracle of what is not yet there, of what is not yet identified."[5] Some of those new selves are relatively healthy, while others become so mired in their indescribable pain that they inflict the trauma they experienced on others. Lot's daughters, especially Zeqenah, seem to have become mired in the traumatic experience of having their own father offer them up for sexual assault and rape. The task of this book is not to scold or critique. Instead, we seek to notice where trauma occurred in some of our most-told stories, to honor the silence around traumatic experiences, and to draw what lessons and healing we can have for our own lives and healing from trauma.

Zeqenah and Qetenah raped Lot. But their sons Moab and Ammon were recognized as Lot's children. Most readers will be squeamish about discussions of incestual rape—I know I am. But a tightly controlled bloodline was seen as a noble feature of national beginnings in some cultures, rather than something to be embarrassed about.[6] Moab and Ammon suffer no shame, and no other biblical texts ever retell the story of Lot and his daughters to mock their national origins.

---

5. Tod Linafelt, *Surviving Lamentations: Catastrophe, Lament, and Protest in the Afterlife of a Biblical Book* (Chicago: University of Chicago Press, 2000), 62.

6. Sarna, *Genesis*, 139.

Rather, Moab and Ammon are remembered simply as Lot's children (Deut 2:9, 19). Indeed, the mention of Ammon and Moab in Deuteronomy seeks to prevent the xenophobic abuse that characterized Sodom's evil. In preventing abuse of foreign flesh, God seeks to halt the trauma and to prevent cycles of pain that perpetuate trauma.

Implications for Ministry

Twelve-step programs begin with the wisdom that realizing that we have hit rock bottom—admitting that something terrible has occurred, keeps occurring, and is likely to continue unless we take drastic steps—is the first step on a long journey away from calamity. Zeqenah and Qetenah insist that we cannot blind ourselves to multigenerational impacts of unhealed trauma. And God offers a model for those who would address sexual violence. It is just going to keep happening unless we stop it. God intervenes to forcefully cease the xenophobic sexual violence.

Just as God sought to prevent the violence of Sodom, God takes great care to insist that the Israelites will not practice the violence to which Lot was willing to subject his daughters. Just in case the reader does not understand how awful Lot was in failing to protect his daughters, the motif of men offering vulnerable women up to a crowd to save themselves is repeated in Judges 19, to devastating effect. The whirlpool of violence and trauma destroys towns and generations of families. So, why is this horrible story even in the text?

The story of Lot and his daughters has two functions. The first is a warning. As Lot physically and culturally moved closer to towns that celebrated abuse of others, especially foreigners, it became increasingly likely that the violence he tolerated would harm his own family and then ultimately himself. Ministry leaders do not dare tolerate and overlook abuse—especially sexual violence—that occurs in or around their communities. Lot's drifting into the orbit of Sodom mirrors far too many Christian churches' and denominations' willingness to tolerate traumatizing behavior, especially if the victims do not line up with societal expectations of who is at risk. Jesus says that for anyone who causes a little one to stumble, it would be better for that person to be tied to a heavy weight and thrown into the depths of the sea to drown (Matt 18:6). There is no level of abuse that is safe to tolerate or can be overlooked in order to "get along." We must not be like Lot in drifting toward the orbit of those who tolerate or practice serial abuse. Lot brought his family with him. Lot and his daughters accepted the terrible lie of Sodom: it is okay to use the sexuality of others for your own gain. We must not accept this lie.

The second function of the story of Lot and his family in Sodom is to lament the impacts of evil. The angelic guests were not the first foreigners to be targeted by the men of Sodom. Lot's married daughters and their families were not the first innocent bystanders to be crushed by the consequences of societal evil. Lot's wife was not the first person to be calcified by grief at the consequences of evil and despair at the toll of cruelty playing out across generations. Lot's daughters were not the last humans to practice the traumatizing violence that was first meted out against them. The biblical text wants you to feel terrible when you read these stories. Lament, especially as felt in the body, is the natural human response to this awfulness. The sick feeling in our stomachs as we read about this evil is a guide that prevents us from allowing further dehumanizing trauma as the cost of being relevant to culture or "not shaming the church." The true shame is tolerating ongoing abuse.

3

DISGUISE AND AUTHENTICITY

Scripture: Genesis 27, 29, 37, 39, 42

> *Now Joseph was the ruler over the land; he was the one who sold grain to all the people of the land. And Joseph's brothers came and bowed down to him with their faces to the ground. When Joseph saw his brothers, he recognized them, but he disguised himself to them and spoke to them harshly. He said to them, "Where have you come from?" And they said, "From the land of Canaan, to buy food."*
>
> *But Joseph had recognized his brothers, although they did not recognize him.*
>
> —Gen 42:6–8

IN A SERMON a few years before his death, Lord Rabbi Jonathan Sacks (may his memory be for a blessing) spoke on parashah *Miketz* (Gen 41:1–44:17) and focused on how Joseph deceived his brothers through his disguise as an Egyptian.[1] Rabbi Sacks placed Joseph's deception into conversation with a tale-type in Genesis of humans using physical disguises to deceive family members to gain something from them. Jacob puts on goatskin and his brother's clothing to receive a blessing from his father, Isaac. Leah puts on wedding clothes and takes her sister's place in the marital bed to gain a husband. Tamar dresses herself in the clothing and veil of a sex worker to be impregnated by her

---

1. For a transcript of his December 10, 2012, sermon, see Jonathan Sacks, "Disguise," Mikketz, 2012–2013, https://rabbisacks.org/covenant-conversation-miketz-disguise/.

father-in-law. And finally, Joseph dresses in Egyptian royal clothes and speaks with the accent/language of an Egyptian to practice authority over his brothers. Rabbi Sacks persuasively argues that, indeed, there seems to be a recurring theme in the patriarchal narratives of family deception through material disguise. In each of these events, those who would be most expected to see through the ruse fail to recognize their own. Further, Rabbi Sacks argues that failure to recognize family in disguise only compounds an earlier failure to recognize the full person:

> *Four scenes, four disguises, four failures to see behind the mask. What do they have in common? Something very striking indeed. It is only by not being recognised that Jacob, Leah, Tamar and Joseph can be recognised, in the sense of attended, taken seriously, heeded. Isaac loves Esau, not Jacob. He loves Rachel, not Leah. Judah thinks of his youngest son, not the plight of Tamar. Joseph is hated by his brothers. Only when they appear as something or someone other than they are can they achieve what they seek—for Jacob, his father's blessing; for Leah, a husband; for Tamar, a son; for Joseph, the non-hostile attention of his brothers. The plight of these four individuals is summed up in a single poignant phrase: "Joseph recognised his brothers, but they did not recognise him."*[2]

Isaac, Jacob, Judah, and the brothers all fail to recognize Jacob, Leah, Tamar, and Joseph—and, pointedly, the difficulties that they have been through—long before the physical disguises are donned or removed.

What Rabbi Sacks did not address in his short sermon was that each of these attempts to disguise themselves is specifically aimed at disguising their gendered bodies. We learn from Judith Butler and others that gender is not a fixed reality; in fact, gender does not exist outside the ways it is performed within a social context.[3] Instead, gender

---

2. Sacks, "Disguise."

3. Judith Butler, *Gender Trouble: Feminism and the Subversion of Identity* (New York: Routledge, 1990), 25.

is performed as a human strategy to fit into societies. So, while Jacob, Leah, Tamar, and Joseph do not change their physical sex in the Genesis text, they do, with varying degrees of success, modulate their gender performance to respond to neglect, abuse, and trauma committed by family members. In each case, they succeed in making themselves literally unrecognizable to those who ought to know them.

Using a performance studies lens to analyze these stories in Genesis highlights how performance can create social realities, mark ethnicity and nationality, realign identities, and stretch cultural repertoires and ethnopoetic rules constraining behavior.[4] Put simply, in the words of Anna Gade: "Performance creates."[5]

But just because performance always creates *something* does not mean that performance creates what the performer intended. The performances of Jacob, Leah, Tamar, and Joseph all go somewhat awry.

---

4. On how performance can create social realities, see Catherine Bell, *Ritual Theory, Ritual Practice* (New York: Oxford University Press, 1992). On how it can mark ethnicity and nationality, see Wynne Maggi, *Our Women Are Free: Gender and Ethnicity in the Hindukush* (Ann Arbor. University of Michigan Press, 2001); Sabra Jean Webber, *Romancing the Real: Folklore and Ethnographic Representation in North Africa* (Philadelphia: University of Pennsylvania Press, 1991). On how it can realign identities, see Joyce Burkhalter Flueckiger, *In Amma's Healing Room: Gender and Vernacular Islam in South Asia* (Bloomington: Indiana University Press, 2006); Lila Abu-Lughod, *Writing Women's Worlds: Bedouin Stories* (Berkeley: University of California Press, 2008). On how it can stretch cultural repertoires and ethnopoetic rules constraining behavior, see Charles L. Briggs, *Competence in Performance: The Creativity of Tradition in Mexicano Verbal Art* (Philadelphia: University of Pennsylvania Press, 1988); Dell Hymes, *"In Vain I Tried to Tell You": Essays in Native American Ethnopoetics* (Philadelphia: University of Pennsylvania Press, 1986); Hans Robert Jauss, *Toward an Aesthetic of Reception*, trans. Timothy Bahti (Minneapolis: University of Minnesota Press, 1982); Dwight Reynolds, *Heroic Poets, Poetic Heroes: The Ethnography of Performance in an Arabic Oral Epic Tradition* (Ithaca, NY: Cornell University Press, 1995).

5. Anna Gade, *Perfection Makes Practice: Learning, Emotion, and the Recited Qur'an in Indonesia* (Honolulu: University of Hawai'i Press, 2004), 49.

They all succeed in making themselves unrecognizable, but they also fail to be truly recognized as who they recreate themselves to be. The healing they hope for from the hurt they have received from family members is incomplete. And yet, even if the outcome of their gendered performance is not what they envisioned for themselves, taking on a material disguise in order to perform their gender differently has profoundly transformative implications for each of the characters in the narrative. The following chapter will focus on Jacob and Leah, with a short discussion of Joseph. The last two chapters will focus on Tamar and return to Joseph.

Jacob

The story of Jacob and Esau is a study in contrasting masculinities. Before her children are born, Rebekah hears from God that one of the nations in her womb will be mightier than the other, and the older will serve the younger (Gen 25:23). And yet, when the children are born, it seems the younger son is destined to serve the older. Esau is born red (*ademoni* as David, 1 Sam 16:12) and also hairy (*sear*, in a repeating reference to Mount *Seir* and the eventual territory of Edom, Esau's descendants. The forested Mount Seir reminded observers of hairy skin). Jacob clings to his brother's heel, but no physical description of him is provided. A ruddy, hairy baby boy that other babies cling to would seem to be destined for greatness.[6] Indeed, Esau becomes the patriarch of a great nation, has multiple wives (Gen 26:34; 28:9) and many children (36:9–19), and forms a kingdom, the text specifically notes, before Israel becomes a monarchy (26:31). Esau is born first, marries first, has children first (probably), and settles a kingdom first through his descendants. But the main focus of the Jacob narrative contrasts Esau's body with that of Jacob.

Esau is an *ish yodea tsid, ish sadeh* ("a man who knew how to trap and a man of the field"), indicating both a level of skill and a preferred

---

6. Egyptian and Cretan art, as well as Ugaritic texts, equate red skin with heroic exploits (see Sarna, *Genesis*, 180).

place of habitation. Esau's body was hairy from birth, to be sure, but it is also shaped by "knowing hunting/trapping" and by being in the field. Hunting needs to be seen as the outlier that it is in the Hebrew Bible. Nimrod (Gen 10:8–9) is the only other hunter mentioned by name in Scripture. Hunting for food was sometimes a necessity if crops failed or if a drought or famine imperiled entire herds and flocks. Certainly, there are rules about what animals can be hunted for food and how they must be eaten (Lev 17:13; Deut 14:5), but only the domesticated cow, sheep, and goat (in addition to birds that thrive in containment) were suitable for sacrifice. Humans may eat wild game, but God was not interested. In any case, hunting for food seems to have been disdained in ancient Israel, and unlike in other surrounding cultures, Israelite kings and nobles are never said to partake in hunting as a sporting diversion. Esau, in embracing hunting as a lifestyle, is presented as a forerunner of his people, the Edomites, and their national god of warfare and hunting, Qaus.[7]

In his backup blessing of Esau, Isaac notes that Esau will live by the sword (Gen 27:40). After Jacob receives Isaac's prime blessing, Esau consoles himself with thoughts of murdering his brother (27:21). It seems that Esau performed violent masculinity, and hunting was just one outlet for the violence. Yet, even when he was not hunting, Esau was habitually in the fields. If even Esau's best garments (27:15) smell like the field (27:27), how much more so his ordinary clothing?

The description of Jacob is a poetic parallel to the description of Esau. Jacob is an *ish tam yoshev ohalim* ("an innocent man who sat in the tents"). The second part of the description, as in the description of Esau earlier in the verse, describes where Jacob spends his time: in the tents. This habitual location has implications for Jacob's embodied reality, too. Certainly, Jacob is physically strong enough to uncover wells that typically take several shepherds to access (29:3, 8, 10), but his body does not seem to ever grow accustomed to the hardships of

---

7. Sarna, *Genesis*, 181.

living out in the fields. Jacob complains to his uncle decades later that the sun scorches him by day and the frost freezes him at night so he is never able to rest (31:40). Jacob's youthful body is shaped by the comfort and protection that goat-hair tents provide.

But just as the first descriptor of Esau in Genesis 25:27 portrays an embodied skill, so too, I argue, does the description of Jacob as an *ish tam* portray him as studied in the art of quietude. Jacob remains devoted to avoiding armed conflict, in sneaking away from Paddan Aram (31:20–21), in placating Esau (32:13–21), and even after the rape of his daughter, Dinah (34:5, 13, 30). Danna Nolan Fewell and David Gunn posit that after Dinah's rape, Jacob is "highly sensitive to the consequences: there is never a final word to violence." They argue, "Jacob's initial silence is wisdom in the face of a potentially explosive situation for his family as a whole. In fact, by avoiding confrontation, he allows the Hivites to offer a potential solution of restitution."[8] The rabbis argue that Jacob was busy in the tents studying the ways of God, while Esau was out looking to procure material gain, frequently through deception—understanding *yodea tsid* as to trap a human in deception (Gen. Rab. 63:10; Tanhuma Toledot 8). Rashi argues that Jacob avoided the violent ways of the world and cultivated innocence/naivete as a skill as a counterpoint to Esau's violent/deceptive quest for acquisition (Rashi on Gen 25:27). Jacob does not go out to seek gain but abstains from acquisitive manhood.[9]

---

8. Danna Nolan Fewell and David Gunn, "Tipping the Balance: Sternberg's Reader and the Rape of Dinah," *JBL* 110, no. 2 (1991): 208.

9. Jacob arguing for marrying Rachel in addition to Leah, as well as the speckled-flock incident, might be brought forward as counterexamples. But in both of these cases, Jacob is only acquiring what he has already earned by mutual agreement with Laban after Laban deceived him. And in searching for a wife from Laban's family, Jacob is consciously obeying his father and mother rather than setting out on his own quest (Gen 27:46–28:4). Similarly, Jacob does not go out to gain Esau's birthright. Instead, Esau comes to him with seemingly nothing to offer in exchange for "red stuff." Jacob only collects what Esau is willing to give.

Just as Jacob's physical body is defined by lacking the toughness that Esau gains by exposure to the outdoors, and Jacob's embodied skill is in eschewing the violence that Esau practices hunting animals, so is Jacob's self-understanding defined by not having what Esau has—Esau is a hairy man, and Jacob is a smooth man. By saying that, however, I do not mean that Jacob is hairless. He has a beard, albeit one that fails to completely cover his neck (27:16). Instead, I argue that Jacob has been shaving at least part of his neck and possibly body hair elsewhere, accentuating the difference between himself and his hairy brother. Jacob is not naturally smooth-skinned. Even in old age, Jacob does not think of himself as bald but gray-haired (42:38). I think Jacob's smoothness, which is not mentioned in the text until Jacob points to it himself, is not a feature of Jacob's body but a choice about how he practices masculinity. In every sense, Jacob performs embodied masculinity as a conscious opposite of Esau. But when the time comes for Isaac to bless his son, Isaac prefers Esau (25:28).

Frequently when we encounter the story of Jacob and Esau in Bibles, the chapter or section title is something like "Jacob's Deception" or "Jacob Steals the Blessing." However, the text presents Rebekah exercising agency and masterminding the deception, then cajoling a reluctant Jacob to participate (27:11–13). Earlier, when Jacob sought to acquire Esau's birthright, he did so transparently and without guile (25:29–34). Selling a bowl of lentils for an agreed-upon price is one thing, but an elaborate deception is another. Jacob is too *tam* to come up with a plan like this on his own or to participate without being pressured. Alicia Ostriker imagines Jacob's self-characterization: "What Jacob's enemies say is that he is smart and charming, a tactician and a skillful bargainer. He admits it. He will also point out that he is extremely competent and scrupulously honest, at least since his youth, unlike some of the people he has to deal with. Since he is not a fighter, no hot-head, he needs these qualities, the virtues suited to states of peace."[10] Jacob does not set out to

---

10. Alicia Suskin Ostriker, *The Nakedness of Our Fathers: Biblical Visions and Revisions* (New Brunswick, NJ: Rutgers University Press, 1997), 95.

deceive anyone. But listening to and obeying his mother are Jacob's most repeated actions in this story (27:8, 13–14, 43, 45), and his mother tells him to deceive his father. After Rebekah and Jacob succeed in deceiving Isaac, Esau pointedly notices that Jacob obeyed their parents (28:7) and decides to try to honor their wishes as well (28:8). However, it is too little, too late. The scene of Rebekah taking the goats that Jacob brought her, killing them, processing the carcasses, cooking them, cleaning the hides, affixing them to Jacob, dressing her son in his brother's clothes, and then "giving the food and bread she cooked into [the] hands of Jacob, her son" (my translation) shows just how active Rebekah is and how passive Jacob, her son, is in planning and preparing for this deception. But to trick Isaac into loving his second son and giving him a blessing, Jacob literally *tries on* the alternative masculinity of his brother. The innocent, smooth man of the tents practices being cunningly deceptive, hairy, and redolent of the fields he disdains.

If Jacob's sudden attempt to perform a masculinity that he had spent his entire life eschewing was not immediately successful, he can be forgiven. After only one word, it seems that the deception fails. Isaac responded to Jacob's first word, "Father," with uncertainty—asking, *Who are you? My son??* (27:18). Jacob's response is to lean into the trap that his mother and he have set for Isaac by completely shedding his innocence and invoking the divine name in misleading his father—"God brought it to me," explaining how he was so quickly able to catch some game. After shedding his characteristic innocence in favor of entrapping his father in a lie, Jacob's voice threatens to give him away. So Jacob presents his goatskin-covered hands to convince his still-uncertain father that Jacob is indeed Esau. The text is explicit that Isaac does not recognize Jacob (27:23). But not recognizing Jacob is not the same as recognizing Esau. Isaac pointedly asks again, "Are you, this, my son Esau?" (27:24, my translation). Rashi notes that Jacob falters at this moment and cannot tell an outright lie but merely responds with the one-word pronoun: "I [am]" (Rashi on Gen 27:24).

With his ears and hands presenting him opposing information about which of his sons is before him, and his eyes useless, Isaac decides to rely on his other senses. Isaac asks to taste the food, which Esau knows how to cook in the way Isaac prefers (27:4). But Rebekah knows how to cook it, as well (27:9), and the food proves inconclusive. Isaac hedges on accepting Jacob's performance of Esau-masculinity. Isaac asks for "my son" rather than "Esau" to come closer so that he can use his sense of smell to finally judge who stands before him (27:26). It is the smell of the fields on Esau's purloined clothing that conclusively convinces Isaac that Esau is before him. Jacob is, after all, one who settles in tents and would never, ever smell like the field.

Jacob must have looked ridiculous wearing goatskins on his arms and neck and his brother's (ill-fitting?) clothing. Jacob apparently can do little to disguise his voice. And despite being a man who spends all his time in the tent-camp, he apparently does not know how to cook meat but only vegetarian food—which Esau cannot even name! (25:30, 34.) Jacob's physical disguise of his embodied masculinity is effective because he feels and smells like the kind of rough outdoorsman his brother is and he is not. Jacob puts off his characteristic innocent/naive masculinity, at his mother's insistence, to deceive his father into loving him and giving him his father's best blessing. In this he is at least partially successful. Isaac does not try to rescind his blessing when he finds out he had been deceived (27:33). Indeed, the next time that the text records Isaac and Jacob speaking with each other, Isaac blesses him again (28:1, 3–4). But the distance between Isaac and his second son, whose performance of gender does not warrant his love (25:28), only seems to have grown. Despite settling back in the land and reconciling with Esau, Jacob returns to see his father only on his deathbed.

After the deception and the trying on of an Esau-type gender performance, Jacob seems to mostly return to type. He certainly acquires a large family, but again, marrying is a command of his parents that he obeys.[11] Subsequent sexual partners are given to him by others (29:23; 30:3–4, 9) though he does not set out to claim them. Yet he also does

---

11. Wilda C. Gafney, *Womanist Midrash: A Reintroduction to the Women of the Torah and the Throne* (Louisville: Westminster John Knox, 2017), 56.

not refuse them. Indeed, Jacob's sexuality seems to be a commodity that his wives feel quite confident and comfortable buying and selling, and Jacob does not refuse this arrangement (30:14, 16–17). If anything, Laban and Leah (and possibly Rachel) conspire to rape Jacob by switching sexual partners without his knowledge or consent. Jacob seems to be an innocent, more comfortable in being acquired than in acquiring.

Rabbinic interpretations of the incident at the fords of the Jabbok further the point of how Jacob has returned to passive, anti-Esau masculinity. The rabbis note that "wrestling" (*wayabeq*) is an odd choice for describing unarmed conflict, and its verbal form only occurs in this chapter. Rashi notes that while other rabbis think the men were wrestling in the dust (*abeq*), he sees something else happening. Rashi understands Jacob and the night visitor's activity as the Aramaic verb "to attach" (*abiq*), as used in Babylonian Talmud Sanhedrin 63b, and the mystery man "attached himself" to Jacob (Rashi on Gen 32:25).[12] Rashi references Genesis Rabbah 77:3 and 78:3 to point out that the "man" is really the guardian angel of Esau, seeking the vengeance that Esau himself will forgo in the morning. Rashi then appeals to Hosea 12:4 to point out that at the Jabbok, there is not just wrestling and overcoming but also "weeping and pleading." The Zohar also focuses on Hosea 12:4 as the basis for an extended discussion about the lack of consent regarding bodily actions between Jacob and the divine being (*lo razah Yakov*) "Jacob did not want it!" Zohar, 3:45a). I argue that what is *suggested* but not mentioned explicitly in this discussion by Rashi and the Zohar is retributive rape. Esau's guardian angel, in Rashi's understanding, performs violent penetration to seek vengeance for Jacob's usurping of Isaac's reward for Esau's violent masculinity.

Yet even in this understanding of the passage, Jacob does not fight off the man but clings to him, asking for a blessing. Ostriker,

---

12. The numbering of this chapter diverges in Jewish and Christian versification. Genesis 32:24 in Christian texts corresponds to Gen 32:25 in Jewish texts.

focusing on the verb *yabeq* as "attaching" and "getting dusty," describes the scene:

> *They stand naked except for their bound genitals. When they begin to wrestle, in the solemn darkness, under the stars, it is chest to chest like straining lovers. Joints grating, they try one grip then another. When they gasp the sound seems blunted by the warm air. Hearing would be impossible for the sleepers in the tents, even if Jacob were to call for help, and he does not think of it. The low moans that they issue appear, again, not to ripple into the atmosphere, but to fall at their feet. They themselves fall to the ground as they grapple. Their sweat mingles, they slip and muddily slide against each other, the skin of each comes to appreciate the slippery volumes of the other. One chest feels the pounding of the other.*[13]

Jacob's habitual gender performance is not a violent, avaricious masculinity but rather its opposite. But Jacob continually seeks to gain blessing and birthright from men who perform and appreciate the results of violence, even when that violence is directed at him. After briefly trying on the gender performance of his brother, Jacob remains an *ish tam*—an innocent/naive man. Nevertheless, Jacob continues longing for the love and approval of his father, and those like him, who appreciate the results of hunting, violence, and deception. Ironically, then, Jacob himself will later deny love to someone desperately seeking it from him.

Leah

Leah's story is a sad, personal tale of unrequited love but also dogged determination and hope. Throughout the tale, Leah tries her best to be the kind of woman that Jacob would desire. At the very beginning

---

13. Ostriker, *Nakedness of Our Fathers*, 98.

of her story, she disguises herself with the help of her family (more on that below) to imitate Rachel and in fact take Rachel's place in Jacob's bed and embrace without his consent or permission. Then Leah spends the rest of her narrative trying to convince Jacob to return to her bed as eagerly as he did when he thought she was Rachel. Leah's material and sensual disguise occurs a scant seven verses after her introduction in the text. When Jacob thinks he is going in to/into his betrothed, Rachel, he goes into Leah instead. The substitution is not evident until the morning. But why is there a substitution at all?

When the text introduces Leah, the narrator notes that Laban has two daughters. The rabbis understood that Laban had two daughters *at the same time* and that Leah was the older of a set of twins, just as Esau was the older of a set of twins (S. Olam Rab. 2). Unlike Esau and Jacob, however, Leah and Rachel were identical twins. When the text says that Rachel "was beautiful of form and beautiful to look at" (29:17, my translation) the same was true of Leah. The difference was that Leah's eyes were רַכּוֹת (*rakot*) or "tender." Many rabbinic sources agree that Leah's eyes were tender because she cried constantly at the thought of marrying her intended: Esau (b. B. Bat. 123a; Tanhuma Vayeze 12; Gen. Rab. 70:16). According to these traditions, Rebekah and her brother Laban sent letters to each other and agreed to have the older twins (Esau and Leah) and younger twins (Jacob and Rachel) marry each other. Naturally, Leah seeks news of her intended husband from passing traders. She hears that Esau is a violent man and deceitful (again, playing on *ish yodea tsid* as one who knows how to lie in wait for/entrap another). As each new report of her intended spouse reveals yet more of his violent masculinity, especially relative to his studious younger brother, Leah weeps more and more until her eyelashes fall out and her eyes are perpetually puffy (b. B. Bat. 123a). Leah is desperate not to marry Esau, and it shows on her face. Jacob, however, is smitten with Rachel from the time he meets—and kisses—her at the well (Gen 29:11). He works seven years for Laban in order to marry

Rachel, and the years pass like the "few days" (29:20) that Rebekah told him to stay in Paddan Aram (27:44).

At the beginning of the seven years, when setting up this contract of a bride for indentured labor, Jacob already displayed awareness that Laban was deceitful. Jacob specified that he would work for Laban's "younger daughter Rachel." In order of the Hebrew wording, Jacob first said "Rachel" to specify who he wanted to marry, "daughter" in case Laban would go to the market and find another woman named Rachel, and "younger," in case Laban would try to change his daughters' names and give him the older one (Gen. Rab. 70:17). Jacob, who grew up with a cunning brother who knew how to entrap others, took steps from the beginning to make sure that Laban gave him Rachel.

Nevertheless, when the wedding day draws closer, Jacob and Rachel know that they cannot trust Laban the deceiver and work out a series of secret signs by which Jacob will know for sure that Rachel is the one in his bed (b. Meg. 13b). But Rachel learns of Laban's deceitful plan to substitute Leah for Rachel.[14] Rachel saw Leah weep for years before Jacob arrived. Rachel has witnessed her older sister continue to mourn her own impending marriage to the violent and treacherous Esau even as Rachel prepares to marry her beloved. Rachel knows that without the secret signs that she and Jacob have practiced, Jacob's refusal will add insult to injury, and Leah will be cast out of Jacob's bed, potentially giving Esau cause to be furious at Leah before they even meet.

Rather than subject her sister to humiliation and fury from both sons of Rebekah, Rachel teaches her identical twin Leah the signs that are meant to prove it is Rachel in the marriage bed. This is why the text is explicit that it is only in the morning that Jacob realized it was Leah, because all (literal) signs pointed to his sexual partner being Rachel (b. B. Bat. 123a). In an achingly poignant midrash, Rachel cares so much

---

14. Jerry Rabow, *The Lost Matriarch: Finding Leah in the Bible and Midrash* (Philadelphia: Jewish Publication Society, 2014), 52.

for her sister that she hides herself among the bed furnishings, and as her intended makes love to her sister and speaks tenderly to her, Rachel cries out in place of Leah's ecstasy and then responds to her beloved's pillow talk to keep up the disguise (Lam. Rab., *petihah* 24).

If Rachel was speaking for Leah, the signs that Rachel taught Leah must have been other-than-verbal passwords. Otherwise, Rachel could have given the spoken responses herself from her position beside the lovers. Indeed, one can imagine easily that Rachel spent hours in the run-up to what should have been her wedding night helping Leah learn all the physical caresses and planned nonverbal responses that Jacob had been dreaming of sharing with Rachel for years (and possibly she with him, though neither the biblical text nor the rabbis discuss Rachel's emotional or sexual interest in Jacob). In this understanding, Rachel and Leah are not enemies. Rather, they love each other more than either loves Jacob, whom they intentionally deceive and therefore submit to sexual violence.[15]

Because of how convincingly Leah is able to mimic the embodied reality of her sister, her performance of the secret signs means that a simple veil is enough of a physical disguise to prevent a man from recognizing her during the sex act and surrounding conversation. After mourning for years about the violent, deceptive man she feared marrying, Leah collaborates with her father and her sister to perform Rachel's embodied sexuality to deceive the "innocent man," Jacob. Her goal is to disguise herself to convince Jacob to excitedly pursue a loving sexual relationship with her. Thanks to Rachel's sacrifice, Leah is successful for an entire night. But in the morning, she can no longer sustain the deception and, behold: Leah!

Unconvinced by Leah's performance that she is capable of emulating Rachel, and no doubt hurt and humiliated by sex to which he did not consent, Jacob finishes the bridal week with Leah, but he still

---

15. Alicia Ostriker has the sisters ask of their interpreters, "Why do they want us to hate each other?" (*Nakedness of Our Fathers*, 105).

loves Rachel more (Gen 29:28, 30). Laban agrees to let Jacob marry Rachel as well, but only in return for seven more years of labor. Jacob knows that as long as he stays in Laban's house and in his father-in-law's service, his marriage with Rachel is in constant danger. Not wanting to upset his deceitful father-in-law, Jacob will fulfill his sexual responsibilities toward Leah until he is free of the family and finally able to divorce Leah. Jacob is now caught in a traumatizing inversion of his experience with Isaac. Rebekah forced her son to deceive his father by giving him exactly what he wanted, in the process obtaining a blessing that Jacob already purchased fairly with a bowl of lentils. Laban forces his daughter to deceive her cousin by raping him, in the process denying him the wife whose bride price he already paid.

God saw this sad situation and how Leah's deceptive performance of Rachel-sexuality had led to a loveless yet still sex-filled marriage. God's apparent solution for Leah's loveless marriage was to give her children while potentially preventing Rachel from having children (Gen 29:31). The rabbis note that Hannah's song (1 Sam 2:5) mentions a woman who was barren but bore seven children, as well as a woman with many children who pines away, and identifies both situations with Leah. She has seven children by Jacob but still pines away for her husband's love. God and Leah decide on a strategy for Leah to win Jacob's affections by bearing children for him. Her naming of her children—Leah, not Jacob, names them—points to her love deficit and her ongoing hope that procreative sexuality will mend what deceptive sexuality spoiled.

Leah's (and Jacob's) firstborn, Reuben, is an embodiment of undisguised hope that Jacob will come to love her (Gen 29:32). The rabbis understood that after the birth of a son, Leah finally felt confident that she would not have to marry Esau. She proclaimed: "Look [at this] son [ראובן, *reuben*]! Esau, the son of Isaac, sold his birthright intentionally, and yet he still sought to kill Jacob. But my son will lose his birthright against his will (because of the incident with Bilhah [Gen 35:22]) but will nevertheless try to save Joseph, rather than be jealous of him (Gen 35:21)" (b. Ber. 7b). According to the rabbinic writings, Leah was given prophetic insights. Knowledge of not only her present situation but also future events shaped Leah's naming of her children.

Similarly, when Simeon is born, Leah notes that the Lord *heard* that she was unloved and has given her another son to make Jacob love her. The next son, Levi, is given to Leah so that Jacob will become attached (*yilaveh*) to her. Leah knows, because of her gift of prophecy, that Jacob will have twelve sons. Having given birth to one-fourth of the sons as one of Jacob's four wives, she feels confident that no one will find fault with her; she has given her full measure of sons (Tanhuma Vayeze 9). Yet even Leah-as-prophet is surprised when she bears Jacob another son. The rabbis understand that Leah gave praise (*aodah*) after her fourth son, instead of her first, because her assumption that each wife would give birth to an equal share of sons for Jacob was incorrect (Gen. Rab. 71:4). Leah can be the best at something! Finally, surely Jacob will again give her the tenderness and desire that she experienced while pretending to be Rachel (Tanhuma Vayeze 9). Leah knows, as well, that her children will be the source of both kings and priests (Gen. Rab. 71:5). Poor, unloved Leah cooperates with God to experience again the love that she experienced on her (sister's) wedding night. But the text is silent about whether Jacob comes to love her because of her fecundity and progeny. In the meantime, Rachel notices that Leah has given birth to many sons for Jacob and becomes jealous, setting off a reproductive arms race between the two formerly compassionate sisters.

The occasion of the mandrakes (Gen 30:14–15) bears special consideration because it illustrates at once Jacob's continued passivity and Leah's continued attempts to have Jacob desire and prize her after his traumatic rejection. Reuben finds mandrakes, a plant known for its aphrodisiacal qualities.[16] Rachel's innocent request for mandrakes meets with Leah's cold rebuff that Rachel took *her* husband. This is the

---

16. Sarna, *Genesis*, 209.

exact opposite of what Rachel engineered with Leah and her father—Rachel gave Leah *her* husband! Nonetheless, Rachel is so desperate for the plants to help increase the potency of her sexual relations with Jacob that she buys them by selling access to Jacob's sexuality for a night. Not content to wait for Jacob to come to the tents, Leah goes out to the husband she shares with three others to claim his sex. Her wording seems almost crude: *elay tabo ki sakor sekartika bedude beni.* Everett Fox's translation is especially coruscating: "You must come into me, for I have hired, yes, hired you for my son's love-apples."[17] Leah does not attempt to disguise that Jacob's preferences are of little importance when the sisters have decided to buy and sell his sexuality. Jacob apparently enters her (tent) without comment.[18]

No longer seeking to entice her husband, Leah has resorted to purchasing his time and sexual intercourse. Leah has never been content to let men have their way with her. Her active and public mourning at being betrothed to Esau was well-known. Her quest to have children who will endear her husband to her demonstrates her agency. And finally, buying her husband's sex demonstrates Leah as herself—in a patriarchal world, Leah has been using what she could to get what she wants. If anything, waiting to *respond* to Jacob when he challenges her to produce the signs on their wedding night is the least Leah-like of her performances in this narrative.

Once more, Jacob impregnates Leah, this time with her sixth son. Leah remarks that God has given her a good gift, in that her husband will finally *yizbeleni* (Gen 30:20). The rabbis disagree on the best way to understand this word. Genesis Rabbah understands *yizbeleni* as something like "he will fertilize me." Leah proudly proclaims that every time Jacob "plows and fertilizes her field," it yields fruit (Gen. Rab. 75:6). Rashi sees this as "he will abide with me," like 1 Kings 8:13, *beit zevel* (a dwelling house). Somehow, Zebulun seems to be

---

17. Everett Fox, *The Five Books of Moses* (New York: Schocken, 1997), 141.
18. Susan Niditch, "Genesis," in *Women's Bible Commentary*, 20th anniversary ed. (Louisville: Westminster John Knox, 2012), 35.

a turning point for Jacob with respect to Leah. She has given him as many sons as the rest of his sexual partners combined. The rabbis understand that at the end of his life, when Jacob was bowing to the "head of his bed" (Gen 47:31), he was bowing to Leah, the head of his bed, his chief wife, and the mother of the plurality of his sons, thanking her for their lives together (Gen. Rab. 71:2).

As a hopeful addendum, the birth of Dinah signals a rapprochement between Leah and Rachel in the rabbinic readings. The younger taught the older to perform sexually in the way that Jacob looked forward to. Leah was always looking for a way to be desired by Jacob the way she was that first night. God's solution is for Leah to endear herself to Jacob through the performance of reproductive femininity. At Leah's success, and at her own failure to have sons for Jacob, Rachel becomes jealous. As she falls further behind in the race to give Jacob sons, Leah begins to feel compassion for her competitor and erstwhile benefactor. When Leah sees that she is pregnant a seventh time, she feels panicked for Rachel. Between her six children and the four of the handmaids, if Leah has a seventh son, there will only be one possible son left before they arrive at the prophesied twelve. Rachel will not have as many sons as even Zilpah and Bilhah.

Leah prays that God will change the sex of the son that she knows she is carrying to be a girl and that Rachel will finally have a son. Genesis 30:21 begins with "and *after this* she bore him a daughter" (my translation). The question logically is raised, after what? It is only after Leah's prayer that the baby's sex is changed to be a girl so that Rachel can bear a son. In the next verse, "God heard her," the "her" is Leah, who prayed for a son for her sister (b. Ber. 60a, Tanhuma Vayeze 19). God honored Leah's judgment (*din*), and so she named her daughter Dinah. Indeed, God seems to honor Leah's judgment throughout the narrative.

Before Jacob made his journey to Paddan Aram, Leah mourned the idea of marrying the older twin, Esau, and wanted instead a man like Jacob. Prior to her wedding night, Rachel acquiesced to the substitution of Leah for herself. Rachel even went so far as to confide in Leah all the secret signs that Jacob had been planning with Rachel for years, ever since Jacob learned that Laban was deceitful. With her sister's help and with a veil, Leah was able to receive all of Jacob's tender kindness and long pent-up desire by convincingly performing wedding-night sexuality as/of her sister. However, when Jacob found out the next morning about the deception played on him by not only Laban and Leah but also Rachel, he was understandably furious. Leah could no longer receive Jacob's love by performing sexuality as Rachel. But she could engage in her own reproductive sexuality—something she, with God's help, was uniquely good at. Leah's deception was short-lived, but the experience of that deception, Jacob's passionate, desirous embrace, she chased for the rest of her life. The rabbis, at least, understood that at the end of Jacob's life, he recognized how much Leah had done for him and that she was and probably always had been his head-wife.

Joseph

Arguably, of the stories in Genesis that describe deception by performing gender differently using disguises, Joseph's is the most profound transformation. In Egypt, Joseph stands over his brothers as they bow to him, clothed in the raiment of Egyptian power, performing ruling masculinity as Pharoah does himself (Gen 42:6–7). Of course the brothers do not recognize him! This is not the Joseph they knew as a child, who straddled boundaries of gender and sex.

Even before Joseph was old enough to make his own decisions about how to use material culture to perform gender, his father made for him a *ketonet passim* (Gen 37:3). I am less concerned with whether it was a "coat of many colors" or a "sleeved garment," and much more concerned with who wears that sort of garment: namely, princesses (1 Sam 13:18). Indeed, the rabbis note that young Joseph is described as beautiful (Gen 39:6) in the exact same way as his mother (29:17) when Jacob first fell in love with her. The garment was part of that beauty. Thomas Mann reasons that the garment originally belonged to Rachel and was in fact her wedding dress. Jacob altered the dress to fit a boy rather than a young adult woman. When Joseph put on the *ketonet passim*, however, his beauty was so reminiscent of his mother that Jacob thought he was beholding his youthful bride.[19] Rachel was a sort of princess as the daughter of a major figure in Paddan Aram. Naturally, she wore a princess dress. When Joseph grew old enough, Jacob made the princess dress into something that Joseph could wear. And the boy looked like his princess-mother on her wedding day.

It is in this garment, dressed up as the favorite wife of their father on their wedding day, that Joseph speaks of his brothers bowing to him someday. When Joseph, who has a history of giving bad reports, comes to check on them, still dressed as the woman that their common father prefers to all their mothers, it is not surprising that the brothers' first action of violence is to strip Joseph of his garment (37:23). Ostriker observes:

> *Joseph is the darling, pretty boy, "fair of form and fair to look at." Those same words having been used to describe Rachel. Joseph is Rachel, somehow, his father's pet: the rabbis say he painted his eyes and walked with mincing step. Showing off the coat of many colors, which old Jacob made him. Twirling, hugging himself. A young Hebrew Narcissus. No wonder his brothers hated him. No wonder they catch him in the field, strip him of his little coat and throw him into the pit, and sell him to Egypt, and rip up the coat and dip it in goat's blood: exhibit A to show the father—do you recognize this coat, dad? A torn veil, a bloody show, a lost innocence.*[20]

---

19. Thomas Mann, *Joseph and His Brothers*, trans. H. T. Loew Porter (New York: Knopf, 1948), 323, referenced in Wendy Zierler, "Joseph(ine), the Singer: The Queer Joseph and Modern Jewish Writers," *NASHIM: A Journal of Jewish Women's Studies and Gender Issues* 24 (2013): 117.

20. Ostriker, *Nakedness of Our Fathers*, 111.

To make sure the reader knows the directionality of the brothers' anger and contempt, the text has an appositive statement: *wayafshitu et-yosef et-kuttaneto et-ketonet hapassim* ("and they stripped Joseph of his tunic, the multicolored tunic"), as if to say, "yes, that garment." The brothers rip up and permanently stain with blood that hated garment, which Rachel and Joseph both wore, because it is the material proof of their inferiority in Jacob's heart.

Joseph does not just dress femininely, however; his actions perform effeminate masculinity as well. The rabbis interpret the repeated mention of Joseph as a *na'ar* to point to Joseph's perpetual immaturity and refusal to grow into postpuberty gender-differentiated roles. Commenting on Genesis 37:2's mention of Joseph as a *na'ar*, Genesis Rabbah notes that Joseph engaged in childish behavior such as penciling his eyes, raising his heel, and curling his hair (Gen. Rab. 84:7). Rashi notes in the commentary on 37:2 that Joseph styled his hair and applied makeup to his eyes. This behavior may seem like a distinctly feminine set of actions to twenty-first-century readers, but eye makeup, especially in desert climates, was and is applied by all genders.[21] Further, Isaac at the age of thirty-seven is also called a *na'ar* (Gen 22:5), so the reference to Joseph's immaturity for the use of this word seems to be out of context. However, when Reuben returns to rescue Joseph out of the pit, he thinks of Joseph as a *yeled* or a young child. Clearly, there was something about Joseph that made him seem young, at least to Reuben and the rabbis.

The rabbis' point that Jacob is young-acting even if he is older in age finds support with Joseph's behavior while looking for his brothers. Joseph is *toeh* in the field when a man comes across him and asks him what he is seeking (Gen 37:15). Typically translated as "wandering," *toeh* carries a potential valence of erring or even being seduced. It is not immediately clear what Joseph was doing in the field, but a man

---

21. See, for example, al-Albani's hadith 633, in which the Prophet Muhammad recommends antimony kohl for improving vision and hair growth.

(Rashi says the angel Gabriel) found him and knew he was wanting something. I argue that Joseph was being youthfully, sexually indiscreet or perhaps just lost focus. Either way, Gabriel arrived to return him to his errand.

In any case, the rabbis' insistence that Joseph is immature followed him to Egypt as well, based on continued descriptions of Joseph as a *na'ar*/young man (Gen 41:12). In commenting on this verse, again, it is imagined that Joseph has been applying eye makeup, styling his hair, and lifting his heel to give others a view of what may be under his garment (Gen. Rab. 87:3). But this time, the midrash also issues a challenge for Joseph. Imaginary observers of Joseph's immature, un-gender-differentiated practices of primping and preening offer an opportunity to prove his manhood—"if you are a heroic man, attack this bear!" (Gen. Rab. 87:3). This is a double entendre and an invitation to another kind of manhood: (1) violent masculinity that asserts itself by hunting animals, and (2) aggressive heterosexual manhood that asserts itself by hunting sex—the bear is understood as Potiphar's wife, who attacked him first, but whom he could "conquer" if he desired.

Against this reputation for prettiness and immaturity, Joseph's performance of Egyptian masculinity stands out in stark relief. As he is being released from prison to appear before Pharoah to interpret royal dreams of cows and corn, the text pauses to inform the reader that Joseph stops to shave and change clothes. Now, Jacob could have paused because Egyptians of the royal court were fastidious and would not tolerate the sight of a prisoner. It could also be that in his rough prison clothes and the beard that had grown, Joseph looked like one of the Hebrew shepherds whom he knew that Egyptians detested (Gen 43:32; 46:34). But it may also be that Joseph just wanted to look pretty again after years in prison. I lean toward the latter interpretation.

After Joseph interprets Pharoah's dream, Pharoah gives Joseph a (nonconsensual?) makeover. Pharoah gives Joseph his signet ring, garments of fine Egyptian linen, and a gold chain around his neck, and has him ride in a chariot in front of which someone calls, *Abrek!*—a word whose meaning puzzles Rashi and earlier interpreters but probably is related to *'b-r.k*, Egyptian for "Attention!"[22] Joseph can no longer be the immature, pretty youth he longed to be but is invested with the clothing, lifestyle, attention, and spouse (41:45) of a serious Egyptian noble.

Joseph was thirty years old when he entered Pharoah's service, and he aged a further seven years (at least) before his brothers saw him again. Joseph had lived in Egypt longer than he had been in Canaan. Due to his position and, I suspect, increasing age, he could no longer perform the youthful, pretty, innocent masculinity that had characterized him growing up. Instead, he was a serious Egyptian court administrator (שליט, "vizier") who held the very survival of Egypt (and surrounding lands) in his hands.

Finally, Joseph's brothers appear before him and bow down. Even though he stands before them, disguised only in Egyptian noble clothing, they do not recognize the man who used to be the seventeen-year-old boy they last saw naked and afraid in a convoy traveling to Egypt. Complicating matters, Joseph speaks to them only in Egyptian, through a translator (Gen 42:23). In this moment, Joseph recognizes them, but they do not recognize him (42:8). The young boy wearing his mother's wedding dress now speaks harshly to them while dressed as an Egyptian man of means and power (42:7).

Like the other disguises discussed above, Joseph's deception is temporarily successful. Unlike Jacob and Leah, Joseph decides when to reveal himself to his family. Certainly Joseph is overcome with emotion and cannot control his sobbing at some points (43:30; 45:2). Nevertheless, Joseph reveals himself to his brothers intentionally, saying simply, "I am Joseph" (45:3).

If Joseph had truly only desired that his brothers would bow to him, he had already achieved that through performing Egyptian masculine authority over them. And yet, I wonder whether Joseph did not

---

22. Sarna, *Genesis*, 287.

want to have his cake and eat it, too: to have his brothers respect and maybe even fear him, but to still be the cute, dolled-up, whimsical man-child he longed to return to being? A hint comes from Jacob's blessing of Joseph at the end of the patriarch's life. In a difficult passage of Hebrew to interpret, Jacob seems to say that daughters/women climb a wall after Joseph's "plant" (Gen 49:22). Targum Pseudo-Jonathan, among others, sees this as a playful reminder to Joseph that even though Jacob is near death, he remembers how Joseph is afraid of or simply uninterested in women and that Egyptian women have been known to try to climb over the walls of his villa to try to seduce him (Tg. Ps.-J. on Gen 49:22).[23] Joseph may be performing Egyptian masculinity in public, but privately Joseph is still sexually immature, never demonstrating the animalistic sex urges that the rabbis imagine to be common to Egyptians (Ezek 23:20). His performance incomplete, Joseph remains afraid of women.

Just as Joseph never grew to love women, Joseph's brothers never came to love him. Isaac still preferred Esau's masculinity. Jacob still preferred Rachel. Tamar did not have a loving, consistent sexual partner. As Rabbi Sacks observes in his sermon: "[Joseph's] brothers no longer hated him but they feared him. Even after his assurances that he bore them no grudge, they still thought he would take revenge on them after their father died [Gen 50:15–18]. What we achieve in disguise is never the love we sought."[24] But, as Joseph insisted repeatedly, his entry into Egypt, and into Egyptian masculinity, was for a blessing for many people (Gen 50:20).

Conclusion

Were the deceptions successful? Did Jacob, Leah, and Joseph get what they wanted? Was their traumatic abuse and neglect healed? Rabbi

---

23. For other ancient authors speculating on women climbing walls, hunting for Joseph's sexuality, see James L. Kugel, *In Potiphar's House: The Interpretive Life of Biblical Texts* (San Francisco: HarperCollins, 1990), 85–87.

24. Sacks, "Disguise."

Sacks does not think so. Jacob wanted his father's recognition of the benefits of his kind of masculinity and the love and blessing that came with it. Leah wanted a loving husband who would pursue her and speak tenderly to her as on her wedding night. Joseph wanted his brothers to respect him or at least not contemplate his murder. Each of the protagonists failed to gain what they sought. And yet, in each case, the deception led to a reinvention of self that was a blessing. Jacob gained the blessing of his father after all and also grew into a patriarch, in every sense. Even after the deception was made clear to Isaac, Jacob received another blessing for his obedience before he left for Paddan Aram. Leah, who was "unloved," became the mother of half the tribes of Israel, including the royal and priestly lines. Near the end of his life, Jacob finally recognized Leah as the head/chief of his bed. And Joseph, though he never truly gained his brothers' respect but only their fear, did gain authority over them and over all of Egypt. They each were blessed through performing alternative expressions of gender and/or sexuality. In Genesis, experimenting with gender performance does not guarantee success by any means. But for Jacob, Leah, and Joseph, at least, performing alternative gender and sexual identities was a path to blessings and healing.

Implications for Ministry

I have been visiting a lot of churches for the first time in the last few years. We have moved a few times, and, as I am an assistant to a bishop, visiting congregations across the Midwest has been a large part of my job. If it is at all possible, the first couple times I visit a congregation I just introduce myself by my first name and try to remain largely anonymous. Part of that is because I am a profound introvert, running on perpetually depleted social batteries. But another part of it, if I am honest, is that churches are not always safe places, especially for folks who work in other expressions of the church. I do not want to have people see me as a representative of a denomination or a synod office before they see me as me: a human with foibles and gifts, with ways I am trying to grow and hurts I am trying to hide. In short, I want to be seen for who I really am, not just for what people ascribe to me. If I must disguise myself a little bit to let my true self have a better chance to show through, so be it.

Jacob, Leah, Tamar (we will return to her later), and Joseph could not be seen for who they were because there were too many assumptions about who they were—and were not. Jacob was not the right kind of man. Leah was the wrong woman. Tamar's sexuality was dangerous for Judah's family. Joseph was just over the top and too much for his family to handle. They all required a disguise to disrupt how their families viewed them to truly be seen for who they were.

How many Jacobs, Leahs, Tamars, and Josephs are in your congregations? Who are the people who are fundamentally misunderstood by those closest to them? The church, as an institution and as a local manifestation of the body of Christ, is to help people dress (metaphorically and literally) in ways that proclaim who they really are. Paul commands those with whom he works to "put on Christ" (Rom 13:14; Gal 3:27). Elsewhere, New Testament authors speak of putting on new selves/natures (see Eph 4:24; Col 3:10). The church is to be intentional at recognizing its role in helping Christians become truly themselves.

This process will, of course, involve multiple steps. The first step always is recognizing which journey must be undertaken. Who is God calling you to be? What mistaken or fraudulent notions of self must be publicly abandoned? And how can the church celebrate the truth of who each person is called to be? Genesis repeatedly demonstrates how putting on a disguise for a short time might be a crucial first step in revealing who we really are.

4

HOLDING SPACE AND RECOGNIZING AGENCY

Scripture: Genesis 34

> *Now Dinah the daughter of Leah, whom she had borne to Jacob, went out to visit the daughters of the land. When Shechem the son of Hamor the Hivite, the prince of the land, saw her, he took her and lay with her and raped her.*
>
> —Genesis 34:1–2

Into the Red Tent

During my first year of my PhD program in Jewish religious cultures, I called my mom just to talk. We discovered that we had both recently read Anita Diamant's *The Red Tent*. My mom was perplexed about why I, a man, had read that book. I explained that aside from loving the genre of biblical romantic fiction, my core academic focus was on Jewish biblical reception and interpretation in situations concerning ethno-religious minorities. The novelization of the narrative of a small clan of outsiders negotiating daily life in the presence of settled people fit neatly within my subject area. Then I asked her why she was surprised that I would have read it. My mom told me that it was a story *for women* about how (some) men ruin love with their misogynistic rulemaking. And, of course, she was right. That is exactly the frame of *The Red Tent*. I asked her whether that was what she saw in the biblical text as well. She answered, "How could I see anything else now? I've heard Dinah's voice."

This chapter will attempt to do exactly what Anita Diamant did for my mother—find Dinah's voice. Patriarchal readings of a patriarchal text reflecting patriarchal cultures have inscribed and reinscribed silence and victimhood on Dinah. Alternative interpretations of Dinah's story—and it must remain Dinah's story—see consent to sex with Shechem, and perhaps even love. Dinah's brothers' violent retribution for sex without *their* consent is the traumatic action in this interpretation. I seek a middle ground, toward a hopeful uplifting of Dinah's agency that stays close to the biblical text and leaves room for a positive outcome, at least for Dinah, if not the Hivites.

A Rape or Not? An Ongoing Argument

At the heart of interpreting Genesis 34, and what happened to Dinah when Shechem "took" her, is the discussion of Dinah's agency and whether she wanted and sought what Shechem did to her. Simply put, did Shechem rape Dinah? The text is not explicit. The text was not written with consent in mind. The focus is on what men *do*, not what women *want*. Susan Niditch observes that Dinah is "absent and present" and "has no dialogue, no voice."[1] She argues that this is a story for men and about men. Dinah is merely the context for a struggle between Israel and Canaan, and the wives and daughters of the men of the city are only a reward for successful trickery.[2] But is the Bible truly unconcerned with the experience of Dinah and the Shechemite women?

Danna Fewell and David Gunn attempt to sympathize with Dinah, and with Shechem, in seeing the two as a loving couple. They see Shechem as a caring lover, approve of Jacob's quietude after he learns of Dinah's abduction, and feel disgusted at the overreach and hypocrisy of Dinah's brothers as they defend their own honor rather than Dinah's person(hood). They argue that Dinah's only possibility

---

1. Niditch, "Genesis," 23.
2. Niditch, "Genesis," 24.

for marriage was in exactly such an arrangement, where a member of the host culture took her. Her brothers do not seem to have any issue taking Canaanite wives for themselves (see Gen 38; 41:45). Why should the reader not perceive a double standard? They argue that, far from being concerned about Dinah's experience or well-being, her brothers are concerned only about her being "defiled," that is, no longer a virgin who could command a high bride price. This understanding neglects, of course, Shechem and Hamor's offer to pay whatever bride price Jacob or his sons name. In any case, Fewell and Gunn do not see the concept of rape in the story but rather a cynical use of "defilement" that Levi and Simeon use as a pretext to first incapacitate and then murder Canaanites who simply supported a man in love. Fewell and Gunn go so far as to say that instead of a rescue when Simeon and Levi take Dinah from Shechem's house, "From Dinah's point of view it is hard to see how their [the brothers'] taking of her is much different from Shechem's taking of her."[3]

Tikva Frymer-Kensky insists that the sexual meaning of the word translated as "afflicted" can point directly to rape, as it does in other stories in the Bible, but that there is nothing in the Dinah story to indicate this is forced sex. Instead, Shechem afflicted Dinah by having sexual relations with her without consent—*which only her male guardian(s), and not she, would have been able to give.*[4]

Johanna Stiebert agrees, seeing Dinah as a pawn in the contest between men. Dinah is the occasion of contest between Israelites and Hivites, and then secondarily between Jacob and his sons about who will decide when and how family honor should be protected.[5] In both cases, the sons of Jacob win the day. But if they win, does Dinah lose?

---

3. Fewell and Gunn, "Tipping the Balance," 206–7, 211.

4. Tikva Frymer-Kensky, "Law and Philosophy: The Case of Sex in the Bible," in *Women in the Hebrew Bible: A Reader*, ed. Alice Bach (New York: Routledge, 1999), 302.

5. Johanna Stiebert, *Fathers and Daughters in the Hebrew Bible* (Oxford: Oxford University Press, 1998), 53.

In her coruscating analysis, Musa Dube applies postcolonial methodology to the Dinah story and perceives Israelite authors describing the Hivites, a soon-to-be colonized people, as both "natives as people with some sexual passions that are uncontrollable" and also "good natives, who love/cling to/adore their potential colonizer."[6] Dube foregrounds the argument of Robert Allen Warrior that people who have experienced colonization and dispossession "will read the biblical text from the perspective of the dispossessed Canaanites."[7] Dube, however, studies how texts construct patriarchal and colonial oppression of the Other from a postcolonial and feminist lens, and accordingly experiences the text from in-between spaces—or a third space. In her reading of the reader, the Other is the Hivite, whom the author paints as a rapacious but eager-to-please colonial subject. A just reading, for Dube, is one that sees the violence not only of Levi and Simeon but also of the writer and reader as we/they other Shechem and his people. Reading rape into the story becomes an act of colonialist dispossession of subjectivity of Shechem, who, after all, loved the girl and (attempted to) speak to her heart (Gen 34:3).

Suzanne Scholz pushes back against those who would paint Shechem as a lover rather than as a rapist. "Biblical scholars mitigated the rape by dwelling on love. Rape could become love; love could incorporate rape. In biblical commentaries, love resulted from rape; in forensic medicine, libido resulted from rape."[8] Scholz argues for

---

6. Musa Dube, "Dinah (Genesis 34) at the Contact Zone: 'Shall Our Sister Become a Whore?,'" in *Feminist Frameworks and The Bible: Power, Ambiguity, and Intersectionality*, ed. Juliana Claassens and Carolyn Sharp (London: Bloomsbury T&T Clark, 2017), 50, 53.

7. Dube, "Dinah (Genesis 34)," 51; Robert Allen Warrior, "A Native American Perspective: Canaanites, Cowboys, and Indians," in *Voices from the Margin: Interpreting the Bible in the Third World*, rev. and exp. 3rd ed., ed. R. S. Sugirtharajah (Maryknoll, NY: Orbis, 2006), 235–41.

8. Suzanne Scholz, "Through Whose Eyes? A 'Right' Reading of Genesis 34," in *Genesis: A Feminist Companion to the Bible*, ed. Athalya Brenner (Sheffield: Sheffield Academic, 1998), 159.

reading what the text says and being honest about what it does not say. After taking, lying with, and afflicting Dinah, Shechem loved her and spoke tenderly to her. The reader simply does not know whether the tender speech reached Dinah in a bed of postcoital bliss or whether she barely heard the words as she lay battered and bleeding in the dirt. Most usefully, Scholz exegetes the verbs of the first three verses of Genesis 34:2 and argues that they point to Shechem's selfishness and disregard for Dinah's humanity, contrary to Fewell and Gunn. In every sense, Shechem is acting on Dinah and doing things *to* her.

In her work "Rape Is Rape Is Rape," Yael Shemesh argues forcefully that wherever the verb *anah* (Gen 34:2; usually "defiled") appears in the *piel* in the biblical text, whether or not it is referring to sexual activity, "the connotation is always negative, involving pressure and distress."[9] Yael Shemesh and Suzanne Scholz see Shechem's clinging to Dinah as exactly what a rapist frequently does to his victim, attempting to pacify, placate and mollify them or somehow convince them that they enjoyed the rape or that it was "not that bad."[10] Simply because Shechem spoke to Dinah's heart does not mean that Dinah's heart was in a position to hear him or that she reciprocated his love.

In her difficult but illuminating work, Rhiannon Graybill insists that the reader stay with the discomfort, trouble, and fuzziness of the account of Shechem's sex acts on Dinah.[11] Graybill insists that the reader remember that there are clearer pictures of rape in the Hebrew Bible (2 Sam 13). We simply do not know, in this account, whether

---

9. Yael Shemesh, "Rape Is Rape Is Rape: The Story of Dinah and Shechem [Genesis 34]," *ZAW* 119 (2007): 5. Shemesh paraphrases Gerstenberger to note that "the verb is used for the application of physical or psychological violence." See E. S. Gerstenberger, "'anah," in *Theologisches Wörterbuch zum Alten Testament* (Stuttgart: Kohlhammer, 1989), 6:253.

10. Shemesh, "Rape Is Rape Is Rape," 4–9; Suzanne Scholz, *Rape Plots: A Feminist Cultural Study of Genesis 34* (New York: Peter Lang, 2000), 141.

11. Rhiannon Graybill. *Texts after Terror: Rape, Sexual Violence, and the Hebrew Bible* (New York: Oxford University Press, 2021), 41, 49.

Dinah consented. And even if she did initially agree to sex, did something turn and the sex became unpleasurable or defiling midway? Sexual encounters are frequently fraught, and consent—agreeing to allow someone do something to someone else—is a profoundly low bar for human sexuality in the first place.[12] Graybill argues that consent is an insufficiently feminist framework and at least partially reinforces rape culture by framing sexual encounters as what a man is allowed to do to a female body.[13] Instead of asking, "Do we think Dinah consciously and explicitly agreed to allow Shechem to take her, to penetrate her, and to afflict her (whatever that meant)?" a good feminist reading should ask, "What did Dinah, as a human with subjectivity, want for herself?" Whatever else is or is not in the text, Dinah was not looking for the encounter with Shechem, so Graybill is inclined to read the story as rape, insisting that we retain the "fuzzy, messy and icky" of the text.[14]

The point of this section is to admit that the text is not explicit—Genesis 34 is not 2 Samuel 13, in which Tamar is explicitly raped by her half-brother. The encounter is fuzzy, messy, and icky. Scholars can and do disagree about what happened to and with Dinah. At the same time, to be acted on and made low, without any thought to or discussion of what one wants, does not sound like a full, healthy sexual relationship.

Finally, though, however we read the story of Dinah—and I insist that we must read the *story of Dinah*, and not just a story with Dinah as a small plot point—Mieke Bal cautions the reader that the biblical interpreter should not "take" and "use" Dinah, repeating the actions of Shechem. Voicing unvoiced women is a "violation of their stories, a subjectification of their objectification, and hence, indirectly, a violence."[15] Even if we claim to love Dinah afterward, we must resist

---

12. Graybill, *Texts after Terror*, 38.
13. Graybill, *Texts after Terror*, 31.
14. Graybill, *Texts after Terror*, 40, 30.
15. Mieke Bal, "Metaphors He Lives By," *Semeia* 61 (1993): 196.

the temptation to put our words in Dinah's mouth and our thoughts in her heart. Especially with this story, we should take care not to use Dinah as a ventriloquist's prop for our own politics. Dinah has already been taken, afflicted, and used as an occasion for a contest between people who may or may not have cared about what Dinah wanted. Any interpretation of her story should be careful not to repeat her affliction. At the same time, Shechem, Jacob, and the brothers, who act and speak throughout the text, seem to be fair game for interpretation and exploration.

Telling the Story

With so much unclear about the story of Dinah, I think it may be useful to tell the tale again, emphasizing certain points from the text. After coming to terms with a pursuing band from Laban, and Jacob's family's fearful encounter with Esau, Jacob is desperate to get away from larger, threatening forces. Jacob misleads his brother about his plans in order to separate from him (Gen 33:12–17). The text notes that Jacob arrived safely in Shechem, indicating that danger was present but avoided (33:18). Still seeking safety for his family, Jacob purchases the land that his wives and children camped on from Hamor, Shechem's father (33:19).

After they are established with a piece of property, Dinah, with her one, clear act of agency, goes out to see the daughters of the land. The text does not say what Dinah saw, but Shechem, the prince of the land, saw Dinah. After the text says he saw her, there are two sets of three verbs that come in rapid succession and sit at the heart of most of the discussion on this passage. Shechem took, laid with, and afflicted (*anah*) Dinah. Immediately after the rape, the second set of three verbs might seem to indicate a change of heart. Shechem's soul clings to Dinah, he loves her, and he speaks (attempted to speak?) to her heart.

Far from the description of Shechem's feelings indicating that the sex was anything like consensual, these sets of verbs make clear that first Shechem has his way with Dinah's body and then he attempts to act on her heart and mind. It is possible that this is a description of innocent love. On the other hand, Rashi, the eleventh-century French sage, insists that Shechem's words are as nakedly acquisitive as his kidnap and rape were before. Rashi, following Genesis Rabbah 80:7, understands that when "speaking to her heart," Shechem said to Dinah, "See how much money your father lavished for a small parcel of land! I will marry you, and then you will acquire the city and its fields" (Rashi on Gen 34:3). Rashi understands that Shechem, not knowing anything about Dinah, assumes that she will be as interested in acquiring property as the people of his city (Gen 34:23). In Rashi's reading, Shechem seems to only be interested in the Israelites when he can take something from them.

We must note that internal logic of the narrative presents the kidnap and rape as an essentially public event. Jacob hears about the incident before Hamor comes to speak to him about acquiring Dinah as a wife for his son (34:5). Likewise, Dinah's brothers hear about the incident while they are still out in the fields with their livestock (34:7). The Hivites apparently waste no time in telling the men of Dinah's family what happened to their daughter/sister. Thus, just after Hamor commences talks with Jacob, the brothers arrive, already informed and burning with anger at how Shechem slept with their sister. The brothers do not seem to repeat among themselves that Dinah was afflicted. That Shechem intended an abduction marriage is offense enough for the brothers to retaliate, even without knowing of the rape act itself.

Hamor and Shechem come to the aggrieved family and offer them a trade for their abducted and raped daughter/sister. Hamor offers the possibility of marriage to Hivite women, and access to the land so that Jacob and his family could buy other portions and move off their one parcel (34:8–10). Shechem is more direct, simply wanting to know how much he should pay for Dinah (34:11–12). Again, the brothers do not seem to know about the afflicting part of the sex act. This unabashed offer to pay to legitimate sex that has already happened is what the brothers claim as their reason for killing the residents of the city. Shechem, prince of the land, treated their sister like a prostitute (34:31). In Israelite culture, and in so many others, paying bride price up front is honorable. Paying for sex afterward is demeaning.

Accordingly, the brothers, without Jacob's knowledge or permission, hatch a plot for revenge. The reader does not initially know what Dinah's brothers have planned, but the author foreshadows that the brothers spoke deceitfully. The brothers offer a "take-it-or-leave-it" proposition. They cannot give their sister or daughters to uncircumcised men. But if the Hivites are willing to circumcise themselves, they could "become one people," and the Hivites would have access not only to Dinah but also all the rest of the women in the small Israelite camp. However, if this idea is unpalatable, the brothers are willing to take their sister and go, apparently without violence (34:13–17). Apparently, the brothers know that returning Dinah to her family voluntarily is not an option for Shechem.

Hamor and Shechem then return to the men of their city and convince them to undergo the painful procedure by promising that they will sweep up all the property (and apparently women) of the isolated and demonstrably vulnerable family (34:23). After all, they mistakenly reason, "These [Israelite] men are friendly toward us!" One wonders whether Hamor and Shechem perceived much friendliness in their meeting with Jacob and his sons while Dinah was ensconced in Shechem's dwelling, or whether they were merely trying to present Israelite friendliness as an inducement for the Hivites to undergo adult circumcision.

The Hivites agree after the promise to acquire all the property of the Israelites, but they are in pain for several days after their circumcisions. Simeon and Levi use the Hivites' discomfort to overpower them and kill the men of the city. We must note the sexual violence, first injuring penises and then killing the whole person. They take Dinah from Shechem's house and leave. Separately, we must emphasize that Dinah's other brothers come to the city filled with all these murdered men and do exactly what the Hivites hoped to do to them: they take all their property, animals, women, and little ones (34:27–29).

When Jacob hears about this, he is furious about the additional danger that Levi and Simeon have brought to his family. So that the reader does not misunderstand, Jacob reminds his sons that their family is small in number and vulnerable. If the people of the land hear of their outrageous behavior, then the clan might easily be wiped out (34:30). The brothers respond that their sister not being treated as a prostitute is more important than the safety of their family.

Jacob's worst fears seem to have come to pass. The surrounding peoples of Canaan seek vengeance on this migrant community that committed extravagantly violent, out-of-proportion revenge for the taking of one of their women. Immediately after the slaughter of the Hivite men, God tells Jacob to leave the small plot of land that he purchased for his family's safe dwelling and travel up to Bethel (35:1). On the way, only a great terror, or a terror from God, keeps the surrounding cities from pursuing Jacob's clan and wiping them out (35:5). After their terrifying flight from another context in which the family might have been slaughtered, Jacob never forgives Simeon and Levi for putting his family in that position. When giving his last blessings to his sons, Jacob recalls the events of Shechem:

> *Simeon and Levi are brothers;*
> *Their swords are implements of violence.*
> *May my soul not enter into their council;*
> *May my glory not be united with their assembly;*
> *For in their anger they killed men,*
> *And in their self-will they lamed oxen.*
> *Cursed be their anger, for it is fierce;*
> *And their wrath, for it is cruel.*
> *I will scatter them in Jacob,*
> *And disperse them among Israel. (Gen 49:5–7)*

Years later in narrative time, Jacob continued to resent how his sons had acted on their own, without his permission, to extract revenge against the Hivites. In the process they brought Dinah back to their camp from Shechem's house, acquired the women and wealth of the Hivites, and made themselves a target for the Canaanites in whose land they were a relatively small migrant community. At no point does Scripture report Jacob's thanks to his sons for rescuing Dinah. Indeed, the patriarch seems to only have focused on the danger his sons' actions brought to the rest of the family. Jacob was apparently willing to trade Dinah to Shechem for continued safety, but the brothers made the opposite trade. Despite their different choices regarding Dinah's predicament, Jacob and his sons were both aware that they were living in a land of people who might kidnap or wipe them out at any moment. Telling their tale and examining their actions and choices within that experience should be central to our reading strategies.

Interpreters have long centralized the precarious position of Dinah and the rest of her family as a small group of vulnerable foreigners. Nachmanides, the great thirteenth-century Spanish sage, links the rape of Dinah with conquest. But Nachmanides posits that the Hivites were trying to conquer the Israelites, not the other way around. He argues specifically that the Hivite men treated the Israelite woman as one treats a war captive: "All forced sexual connection is called 'affliction.' Likewise, [citing Deut 21:14, the case of a woman captured in war whom a man takes as a wife] 'Thou shalt not deal with her cruelly, because you have afflicted her.' . . . Scripture thus tells—in Dinah's praise—that she was forced, and she did not consent to the prince of the country."[16] In the relevant law that Nachmanides cites, Israelite men had to wait one month after capturing a woman in war before having sexual contact with the woman.

This is a difficult law to appreciate, to be sure. Yet, it marks a massive sea change from limitless acquisitive rape after combat. Simply enforcing "don't rape captives" (and do not take them in the first place) would be better, of course. This law had that as its goal, however. The Israelite man had to give the captive time to grieve her

---

16. Nahmanides, *Commentary on the Torah: Genesis*, trans. Charles B. Chavel (New York: Shilo, 1971), 413–14.

parents, and additionally had her cut her hair, grow her fingernails, and remove her foreign clothing. Rashi argues that all this was done so that the man would not be able to find her exotic or attractive and would eventually decide to not have sexual relations with her during the month delay (Rashi on Deut 24:12–13). If the man decided to pursue sexual relations anyway, and if the captive woman did not please him, she was to be set free *because he afflicted her*. If a woman were taken captive by a member of a stronger force who then had sex with her, Nachmanides insists that, even in the *relatively* (and this "relatively" is doing a lot of work!) humane case of the Israelites capturing potential wives, the situation was to always be regarded as nonconsensual sexual contact.

Indeed, the abduction and separation of Dinah from her family is an important part of Shechem's and the Hivites' plans. Joseph Fleishman notes that Shechem saw Dinah in the company of the daughters of the land, probably at a festival where women assembled to dance. This situation was often the site of kidnapping women for nonconsensual sex (see Judg 21:19). Fleishman suggests, "[Shechem] abducted [Dinah], apparently with the help of his friends, and had sexual relations with her at some place. . . . It is very likely that Shechem decided to abduct Dinah for purposes of marriage because he was aware of Jacob's separatism, and expected Jacob not to consent to such a marriage."[17] Abduction and affliction, and then attempting to smooth over the actions by offers of money (Gen 34:12), are not the actions of a population overpowered by colonial forces or influence or infatuation with their colonizers. Instead, the prince of the land takes a woman and then, *after* having sex with her, bargains with her father for her without so much as an apology or an offer of return. This is an expression of contempt that only the powerful citizen can have for the powerless foreigner.

---

17. Jacob Fleishman, "Shechem and Dinah—In Light of Non-biblical and Biblical Sources," *ZAW* 116 (2004): 27–28.

Returning to Dinah's Agency

But, again, we return to the question: Who speaks for Dinah? Shechem, the prince of the land who took, laid with, and afflicted Dinah, must not be the one who speaks for her. Jacob and the brothers all speak for themselves and their own ideas of what is right. In a quest for Dinah's agency, we must turn to her actions. As noted earlier, Dinah does not speak in this text, but she does act. To respond to Spivak's famous question "Can the subaltern speak?" we must see Dinah's voice in her agency and in her actions.[18]

Dinah's agency is displayed most clearly in the opening verse of the chapter: "Now Dinah the daughter of Leah, whom she had borne to Jacob, went out to visit the daughters of the land" (Gen 34:1). Leah's mention here and absence in the remainder of the story centered on her daughter's experience is noteworthy and frequent grounds for interpretation.[19] Rabbinic interpretation of Dinah's actions and desires focuses on her introduction as the daughter of Leah instead of the daughter of (just) Jacob. Leah purchased for herself her husband's sexuality with the sale of her son Reuben's mandrakes to her sister, and Rachel sold a night with Jacob to Leah (30:14–16). To collect her reward, Leah went out (*tetse*) to meet Jacob as he returned from the field, to claim him as a sexual partner for the night. The rabbis understood that when Dinah, the daughter of Leah, "went out," she was also looking to claim a sexual partner (Gen. Rab. 80:1). To bolster the point, Genesis Rabbah quotes a contextualized proverb from Ezekiel 16:44, saying, "If the mother pursues lewdness, so will the daughter." Yosi of Me'ona goes so far as to say, "Leah went out dressed as a whore, and therefore Dinah the daughter of Leah went out [Dinah went out also dressed as a whore]"

---

18. Gayatri Chakravorty Spivak, "Can the Subaltern Speak?," in *Marxism and the Interpretation of Culture*, ed. Cary Nelson and Lawrence Grossberg (Urbana: University of Illinois Press, 1988), 271–313.

19. Julie Kelso, "Reading the Silence of Women in Genesis 34," in *The Bible, Gender, and Sexuality: Critical Readings*, ed. Rhiannon Graybill and Lynn R. Huber (London: T&T Clark, 2021), 19.

(Gen. Rab. 80:1). "But what was she wearing . . . ?" is as ancient as Bible interpretation, we see, and at least some of the rabbinic interpreters see what happened to Dinah as her own fault for being too much like her mother.

Yet where Leah went to find her husband for permissible, marital sex, the rabbis imagine that Dinah was looking for something else and that she found what she was looking for with Shechem. Genesis Rabbah 80:5 addresses the multitude of verbs in Genesis 34:2 to say that Shechem took Dinah to be his sexual partner, lay with her "in the natural way" (i.e., vaginal intercourse), and afflicted her by having sex in an "unnatural way" (i.e., anal sex). Elsewhere, Rashi, relying on Genesis Rabbah, insists that the gentile Canaanites were famous for preserving vaginal virginity of young women by practicing anal sex (Rashi on Gen. 24:16). Some rabbinic interpreters imagine that Dinah did far more than consent; she pursued and enjoyed defiling sex. Rabbi Yudin says that the brothers had to drag Dinah away from Shechem's house because she was desperate to stay with him, and Rabbi Chonya adds, "Once a woman has had sex with an uncircumcised man [in the way of gentiles, discussed above], it is difficult for her to separate from him" (Gen. Rab. 80:11).[20] The rabbis see Dinah as pursuing and then clinging to the possibility of the defiling sex she went out to find in the first place.

These interpretations in which Dinah is completely to blame for what happened to her are furthering two goals for their interpretive communities. The first is to control and limit the behavior of women. "Don't go out among strange men, and don't wear anything slutty, or you are just asking for it . . . like Dinah!" The second goal is to absolve Jacob for not seeking to redeem his daughter.

And yet, all these interpretations completely neglect the objective of Dinah's "going out" in the text. Dinah went out to see "the daughters of the land" (Gen 34:1). This is Dinah's action that she took

---

20. As discussed in Alison L. Joseph, "Who Is the Victim in the Dinah Story?," TheTorah.com, 2017, https://www.thetorah.com/article/who-is-the-victim-in-the-dinah-story.

under her own agency. If Genesis Rabbah is correctly interpreting the link between Leah's "going out" for sex and the close grouping of Dinah going out and the reminder that she is Leah's daughter, was Dinah interested in seeing and "knowing" the Hivite women? Jane Everhart asserts that Dinah's going out to see the women of the land is an unsubtle description of Dinah's quest for a female romantic/sexual mate.[21] I think this approach is closest to the text while taking seriously the strong intertextual links with Leah going out for sex. This reading also has the benefit of taking Dinah's agency and desires seriously, as Graybill insists a good, feminist reading must.

If Dinah's choice and sole self-directed action in the text was to look for women in the land with whom she could be intimate, this changes not only how we interpret Dinah's experience of Shechem taking her but also Shechem's motivation. Shechem took Dinah, lay with her, and afflicted her. It was only after he had sex with her that Shechem's soul clung to her, he loved her, and he spoke to her heart. His feeling for her came *after* the sex acts he did to her, not before. I argue that this describes not only rape but so-called corrective rape, when a man sexually assaults a woman he suspects is not heterosexual in an attempt to change her sexuality.[22] Similarly to Genesis 34:2, Charlayne Hunter-Gault uses the term "defiled" to express the precise goal of "corrective rape."[23] The perpetrator attempts to defile or

---

21. Jane Everhart, "Women Who Love Women Reading Hebrew Bible Texts: About a Lesbian Biblical Hermeneutic," in *Feminist Interpretation of the Hebrew Bible in Retrospect*, vol. 2, *Social Locations*, ed. Suzanne Scholz (Sheffield: Sheffield Phoenix, 2014), 200.

22. See Kemone S-G Brown, *When Rape Becomes Acceptable: Corrective Rape in Jamaica* (Kingston: Tamarind Hill, 2017); René Koraan and Allison Geduld, "'Corrective Rape' of Lesbians in the Era of Transformative Constitutionalism in South Africa," *Potchefstroom Electronic Law Journal* 18, no. 5 (2015): 1930–52.

23. Charlayne Hunter-Gault, *Corrective Rape: Discrimination, Assault, Sexual Violence, and Murder against South Africa's L.G.B.T. Community* (Chicago: Agate Digital, 2015), i.

afflict the victim such that she can no longer practice her problematic sexuality—in the view of the rapist—and will somehow be forced into heterosexuality. Sexual trauma is precisely the goal for the "corrective" rapist.

According to this interpretative lens, when Shechem saw a woman, an ethno-religious minority and newly arrived migrant, take a bit too much of an interest in the daughters of *his* land, he acted. After he tried to rape her interest in women out of her, Shechem developed feelings for her. Yet, he could never allow Dinah to return to or even speak with her family, fearing that she might voice her unwillingness to be married to her rapist or any man, for that matter.

Conclusion

Ultimately, we do not know whether Shechem's affliction of Dinah was an attempt at "corrective rape." Further, we do not know whether Dinah was sexually interested in the daughters of the land, however much support that opinion has in an intertextual reading. What is clear is that even in a story in which she does not speak, Dinah still has preferences and agency. She went out to see the women of the land to which she had come. Scripture is silent on whether she encountered them before Shechem took her. But after her brothers took captive all the women and little ones of the city and brought them into the Israelite camp, Dinah finally had the opportunity to do that which she chose to do at the beginning of this story: see and interact with the women of the land. I hope that, after her rape at the hands of Shechem and violent retribution of her brothers, she at last found what she was looking for among the women of Canaan.

Implications for Ministry

The name of this chapter includes the phrase "holding space," because that is what Dinah's story demands of us. Graybill insists that we stay with the fuzzy, messy, and icky in the text and not rush to remove discomfort or uncertainty. All too often, we draw one interpretive meaning from biblical texts and then tie them up with a bow and move on. We do the same with interpersonal trauma and abuse in our communities. Without knowing all the facts, we conclude that this person is all right, that person is all wrong, and that's it. Some interpreters see Shechem as the victim of proto-conquerors. Some see Dinah as the victim of rape, xenophobia, and homophobia. Having read this chapter, you know my sensibilities. What do you think?

More important than any of that, though, is what did Dinah think? What did Dinah experience? And what of the Hivites and the victims of Simeon's and Levi's disproportionate revenge? If nothing else, please practice what so many interpreters do not: hold space for those most affected to demonstrate what they want—and do not want—after trauma and abuse. There is no one-size-fits-all trauma response. The self that trauma obliterates is the self that needs to be rebuilt and reintroduced to itself.

Good trauma care is gentle, slow, and focused on the needs of the victim(s). Otherwise we risk retraumatizing victims by reinscribing the forcefulness of others overpowering the selfhood and subjectivity of the victim. Dinah knew what she wanted all along, even if Shechem, Jacob, Levi, and Simeon failed to ask her. The next chapter seeks to allow Dinah to speak for herself.

5

THE TRAUMA OF JOB'S WIFE

Scripture: Job 2

Then his wife said to him, "Do you still hold firm your integrity? ברך *God and die!"*

—Job 2:9, my translation

Introduction

Stepping outside the patriarchal narratives of Genesis, I want to consider the case of Job's wife. Her story is a continuation of the gendered family trauma we have been exploring. That would be enough reason for this brief foray outside Genesis. But Job's wife is traditionally understood to be Dinah, the daughter of Jacob. To continue her story and consider her words (at last!), we contemplate her role in the book of Job, particularly as she offers advice for dealing with trauma.

This story centers men, men's advice, and male suffering, and gives a grieving mother only a couple words of speech, notably to her husband, saying nothing about her own experience. Job's wife, more than any other character in the book, however, seems to know what God is thinking. In her brief speech in 2:9, Job's wife echoes the words of God in Job 2:3. She and God both know that Job has maintained his integrity (*tummah*). The history of interpretation has not been kind to this woman who echoed God. Church fathers and rabbis alike have seen her as a source of temptation for the book's eponymous protagonist. But I would like to stress an interpretive tradition that lifts up Job's wife as one who is uniquely qualified to make sense of Job's—and her own—traumatic experience. In so doing, Job's wife echoes both the speech and actions of God.

Temptation

There is a long tradition that sees Job's wife as an arch-temptress when she induces Job to "curse" God and die (Job 2:9). If she were somehow sinful here, she would certainly have ample reasons to want to defy God. The satan[1] has touched flesh and bones that belong to her in a way that Job can never understand. In the sudden, violent death of her children, as well as the mutilation of her husband's flesh, the wife of Job experiences suffering every bit as traumatic as that of Job. That her own body is not apparently the locus of suffering is largely beside the point. The bodies of her children, created within her own self, have been destroyed, buried without even a funeral or a final goodbye (Job 1:19). The body of her husband is disfigured and repulsive. If Job is bitter, Job's wife has just as much right to bitterness, if not more. We do not know of any friends who come to comfort her. Her own husband lashes out at her. And she presumably never hears directly from God, as did Job, to satisfy her gnawing grief. Job's wife's horrifying experience would seem to be fertile ground for anger and sin.

Many interpreters, particularly Christians, have found in Job's wife's brief words the evils of sin and temptation. Origen understood Job as a prepatriarchic analogue of Christ, who was not bound by the Mosaic law (which had not yet been revealed) but nonetheless lived without sin. Just as Christ was led into the desert to be tempted by the devil, so was Job led into his house to be tempted to sin by his

---

1. A note on naming: The book of Job continually uses "the satan" (הַשָּׂטָן) to describe the other character in this divine wager. Readers should not understand the satan as a personification of a power opposed to God here, or as the Christian notion of Satan. Instead, the satan is one of God's agents in the world, who is very much welcome in the divine court, and whose job is to seek out and test humans on God's behalf. I use "the satan" to reflect the Hebrew usage and meaning in Job.

wife.² Chrysostom saw Job as a second Adam who was an opposite of the first. As Adam was tempted by the snake in paradise (Chrysostom does not mention Eve as tempter), Job was tempted by his wife while sitting on a dunghill.³ Whereas Adam was tempted by a foul creature while in paradise and should have had an easy time recognizing and refusing temptation, Job was tempted by his lover while in terrible suffering, and presumably the temptation would have been more difficult to endure. Nevertheless, Job succeeded where Adam failed. Augustine famously thought of Job's wife as the *adiutrix diaboli*, "the helpmeet of the devil."⁴ Where the satan tempts Job to turn against God indirectly by causing him suffering, Augustine reads Job's wife as directly inducing him to sin through cursing God. John Calvin considered Job's wife "an instrument of Satan . . . a she-devil . . . a fiend of hell."⁵

Christian interpreters, reading translations that invert her words, imagine Job's wife saying, "Do you still hold on to your fear of God? Do you still bless God? . . . That is now a futile act. It does not pay. Give up your piety; curse God and die."⁶ Later interpreters, struggling with how Job could bless God with integrity even after the deaths of his children, read Job's wife's words as a challenge: "Do you still possess your integrity as an individual? . . . Are you not in danger of 'bad faith' in alienating yourself from yourself by this disgusting display of fawning religiosity? If you really want to keep a grip (*mahziq*) on your integrity (*tumah*) . . . you will curse (*brk*) God, even if it means you die."⁷ In this reading, Job's wife questions whether he can hold on (*mahaziq*) to his *tummah* if he *does not* curse God and die. This, however, is reading against the text.

---

2. C. L. Seow, *Job 1–21: Interpretation and Commentary* (Grand Rapids: Eerdmans, 2013), 169.
3. Seow, *Job 1–21*, 175.
4. J. Gerald Janzen, *Job* (Atlanta: John Knox, 1985), 49.
5. Seow, *Job 1–21*, 305.
6. Janzen, *Job*, 50.
7. Janzen, *Job*, 50.

Interpretations of Job's wife as a temptress are not the sole preserve of Christians. In one early midrash, Job's wife is considered a sort of unsuccessful proto-temptress, as in Chrysostom's interpretation. Job has learned from Adam that he should not accept what his wife offers him. Job says, "I am not like Adam. He listened to his wife, and sinned by eating of the Tree of Knowledge. But I did not heed my wife, I did not curse the Lord, and I did not sin" (Gen. Rab. 19:12). In the circle that produced this midrash, *brk* was also read as a euphemism for "curse," and Job's wife was seen as counseling blasphemy. Alternative Jewish traditions, however, offer a more nuanced picture of Job's wife that allows the text to speak without reversing common meanings.

Ambiguity of "Bless"

In most English translations of Job's wife's suggestion in Job 2:9, the Hebrew root *brk* is rendered as "curse." Even a footnote reflecting that Hebrew texts read "bless" here leaves the casual reader confused as to how a word can mean its opposite. The Syriac Peshitta is the only ancient translation that renders the verb as "curse": "*sh' l'lwh wmwt / revile God and die!*" even as the Targum Job retains "bless."[8] The oldest Greek texts of Job (which themselves are greatly expanded), say *eipon ti rhema eis kyrion / "say something* to the Lord."[9] The Vulgate, however, translates the passage literally as "bless." Still, Luther, Calvin, and KJV all render the verb "curse."

Some argue that "bless" here functions as a euphemism for "curse" because the ancient authors were too concerned with God's honor to insert a curse into Job's mouth. That reading does not make sense, considering Job's speech toward God in the rest of the book of Job.[10] The twin assumptions that cursing is the only appropriate

---

8. Seow, *Job 1–21*, 305.

9. Seow, *Job 1–21*, 305, emphasis added.

10. Gudrun Elisabeth Lier, "Translating ברך in Job 2:9—A Functionalist Approach," *AcT* 38, no. 2 (2018): 105–22.

response to God's (in)actions and that the author(s) of Job had a discomfort with cursing God seem to be a later development that should not be retroactively inserted into Scripture.

I argue that we should read *brk* as it is used everywhere else in the Hebrew Bible: "to bless."[11] But for what reason would Job's wife counsel her husband to bless God and die? Choon-Leong Seow argues that Job's wife may be expressing a positive intent to bless God for four different reasons.[12] The first reason is that she may simply be encouraging Job to bless God as a final act before he dies, as a sort of goodbye to life. In the scope of Job's experience thus far, his fortunes and family have been taken from him, and then his health has seriously suffered. All indications are that he may soon die himself. Saying a final closing prayer before an imminent death may be Job's most pious option.

Second, Job's wife may be encouraging him to refuse to play God's game (if she has a sense, indeed, that there is a game afoot). By blessing and dying, Job would remove himself from the equation, retaining his integrity but removing himself as a pawn in the struggle between the satan and God. This is probably the sense in which the satan predicts that Job will "bless" God.

The third interpretation of Job's wife's incitement to blessing is closely related to the first. Not knowing whether Job's life is ending, his wife encourages him to continue his pious life for as long as he has

---

11. Francis Anderson rightly argues that 1 Kgs 21:10, 13 and Ps 10:3 are specific economic instances where an oath has been sealed by blessing God, and yet the seller has refused to follow through with the agreed-upon deal. Simply "cursing" God (and Ahab) in the 1 Kgs 21 context makes no sense. However, blessing God's name (and Ahab's) to seal a deal, and then refusing to sell the field, as the scoundrels accused him of, was taking the Lord's name in vain. Similarly, Ps 10:3 speaks of a greedy man who blesses God but then shows disrespect to God by not honoring his financial obligation supported by the invocation of the divine name. The greediness of the man is central to understanding what was happening. See Francis I. Anderson, "The Socio-juridical Background of the Naboth Incident," *JBL* 85, no. 1 (1966): 46–57.

12. Seow, *Job 1–21*, 305.

it. She says, in effect, "Continue to bless God as you always have, and [eventually] you will die [and this suffering will be over]."

The fourth and most reasonable interpretive possibility sees Job's wife as filled with pity and desiring to bring an end to Job's suffering. The blessing that she counsels Job to make is a request for God to make a reciprocal blessing on Job: the blessing of death. Blessing God in thanks for, or petition for, a reciprocal blessing is a frequent feature in the Hebrew Bible.[13] Job's wife argues that Job has done enough in his life, and in the face of so much suffering, God will surely be faithful to loyal and pious Job and grant his request of a quick death, leaving Job's wife to her apparently more manageable grief.

Whatever the intention behind Job's wife's words, they are clearly important to Job. Within a few verses of seemingly rebuking his wife (see below), Job seems to be following her advice, at least with regard to petitioning God for death.[14] Job alludes to a preference for death:

> *Why is light given to one burdened with grief,*
> *And life to the bitter in soul,*
> *Who long for death, but there is none,*
> *And dig for it more than for hidden treasures;*
> *Who are filled with jubilation,*
> *And rejoice when they find the grave? (Job 3:20–22)*

Job then directly petitions God for death:

> *Oh, that my request might come to pass,*
> *And that God would grant my hope!*
> *Oh, that God would decide to crush me,*

---

13. Christopher Wright Mitchel, *The Meaning of BRK "To Bless" in the Old Testament*, SBLDS 95 (Atlanta: Scholars Press, 1987), 169–71.

14. Alan Cooper, "The Sense of the Book of Job," *Prooftexts* 17, no. 3 (1997): 233.

> *That He would let loose His hand and cut me off!*
> *(Job 6:8–9)*

Job has fully accepted his wife's counsel for him to embrace death as he petitions the Lord for an end to his suffering.[15]

Further, if Job is content to accept evil as well as good from the hands of the Lord (Job 2:10), as a simple reading of his reply to his wife would suggest, then on what basis does Job conduct his argument that God has unfairly repaid him evil for good in the following chapters? Just as I argue that Job's wife is not counseling blasphemy but rather encouraging Job to bless God, I argue that Job cannot be simply accusing his wife of foolishness and telling her to accept the bad with the good.

A Trauma Specialist's Response to Tragedy

Anticipating his own death, Job has already blessed God (Job 1:21) by the time his wife advises him to do it again.[16] Job's wife assumes that it is only his fight for his integrity that is keeping him alive and suffering. Her advice, in this reading, is for him to continue to hew to the path that he has seemingly already chosen, to bless God and prepare for his impending death. Job rebuffs her, however. Job will not go silently into the night but will continue his fight to preserve his innocence and integrity. Then Job utters the words that characterize his wife for all the time: "You speak as any *nebalot* speaks" (2:10, my translation). This word, *nebalot*, provides the basis for a rabbinic rehabilitation of Job's wife's character.

---

15. Lyn M. Bechtel, "The Development of Job: Mrs. Job as Catalyst," in *Feminist Companion to Wisdom Literature*, ed. A. Brenner (Sheffield: Sheffield Academic, 1995), 201–21.

16. William Brown, *Wisdom's Wonder: Character, Creature and Crisis in the Bible's Wisdom Literature* (Grand Rapids: Eerdmans, 2014), 74.

Nebalah has frequently been translated as "foolish" (LXX, Vul, Pesh).[17] This translation is insufficient to capture the notion of the commission of a serious, social fault. The term does not describe someone who (only) lacks mental acuity but rather someone whose life or actions demonstrate a willful breach of ethics or customs. Isaiah describes how *nbl* is intimately linked to ungodly behavior:

> *The* nabal *speaks* nebalah,
> *And his heart inclines toward wickedness:*
> *To practice ungodliness and to speak error against the* LORD,
> *To keep the hungry person unsatisfied*
> *And to withhold drink from the thirsty. (Isa 32:6)*

Speaking *nebalah* is inseparable from practicing ungodliness, depriving neighbors, and saying things that are untrue of God. In a classic example of a social outrage, Nabal (who is named according to his outrageous behavior), the husband of Abigail, refuses David's request of provision on a feast day after David had provided safety for Nabal's shepherds (1 Sam 25:2–25). This violation of expectations of hospitality and reciprocity has fatal consequences for Nabal. Flouting convention, harming others, and misrepresenting God are all at the root of *nbl*. In a sense, after Job brings up the *nebalot* in conversation with his wife, the rest of the dialogue with his friends is one extended discussion on who is committing *nebalah*: Job, his friends, or God.

In the scope of the biblical canon, one of the most serious forms of ethical outrage is the offense against a person's body, frequently through sexuality. The woman who fraudulently passes herself as a virgin at the time of her marriage, bringing dishonor on her father, who misrepresents her to her husband, has committed an outrage/*nebalah* (Deut 22:13–21). But it is the rape of an Israelite woman that is the paradigmatic outrage. Tamar warns that rape by her brother is *nebalah*

---

17. Seow, *Job 1–21*, 305.

and that if he goes through with it, he will be regarded as one of the *nebalim*/outrageous ones (2 Sam 13:12–13). Earlier, the brothers of Dinah lament that their sister has been defiled by Shechem and that an outrage/*nebalah* has been done in/to Israel (Gen 34:7).

The rabbis note the use of the root *nbl* in Genesis 34 and Job 2 and suppose an intertextual linkage between Job's wife and Dinah. Recognizing the implied setting of the book of Job in the time of the patriarchs, and that the expounding of Job's wealth of children and animals situates him as a patriarch himself, the rabbis teach that Job's wife *is* Dinah, the daughter of Leah and Jacob. Job's description of his wife's words as like those of the *nebalot* reflects her earlier traumatic experience with Shechem (b. B. Bat. 15b; Gen. Rab. 19:12). Dinah's body has been the locus of ethical and social outrage. The rabbis recognize that she speaks from the position of one familiar with communal trauma. For this reason, the Aramaic Targum explicitly names Dinah as Job's wife in 2:9.

As one who had already experienced a tremendous outrage against her person and whose body was the object of abuse and trauma by an outside power, Job's wife, Dinah, had years of experience coping with just the sort of trauma that Job was now facing for the first time. Her response is not, in this reading, evil, and it certainly is not "foolish." Instead, she advises him, out of her deep anguish at losing her children and seeing her husband tormented, and compounded by her memory of her own violation, to die quickly but faithfully, lest he undo his blamelessness.

A short, surviving excerpt of Midrash Iyyob has Dinah say, "You are unable to survive all this misery and sorrow. It will lead to the loss of your integrity. It is preferable to bless God and die, in order to leave this world innocent, exemplary and virtuous, and not sin" (Midrash Iyyob 14). Her question, "Do you still grasp your integrity?" must have been asked with concern mixed with awe. Dinah does not act as the satan's helpmate, but rather she seeks to preserve her husband's innocence and character, which are so precious to him, while at the same time bringing an end to his suffering. Having lost her children, Dinah is willing to part with her husband to ensure that he does not experience the greatest impact of trauma—a loss of self.

In this interpretive tradition, Job's response to his wife is not the cold rebuke of a husband who does not care for his wife's suffering. Instead, he recognizes that Dinah is speaking as a member of the terrible sorority of those who have experienced horrible trauma. Job knows and remembers the pain that Dinah suffered and from which she speaks. He reminds her, perhaps not as gently as we would like, that the lot of humanity is to accept good as well as evil from the hand of God. This can even be read as a sort of hopefulness. Dinah is well acquainted with evil throughout her life, and it has returned to her and her family. But Job reminds her that, even amid their/her suffering, they have received good from God, as well. It might have been cold comfort as she stared at her disfigured husband and longed to embrace the bodies of her children. But perhaps remembering that they had received good along with evil was simply the best that they both could do at the moment.

Giving Birth

Job and Dinah emerge from their shared suffering at the end of the book, and they practice hope. This is an area, I believe, where Job's wife directly emulates God. In the whirlwind speeches, God pointedly speaks of God's delight in the ostrich (39:13–18). Perhaps cruelly, God points out that the ostrich may forget where she has laid her eggs and crush her unhatched children in her forgetfulness. Job and Dinah have suffered the crushing deaths of their children and certainly have not forgotten them. This reference to the careless ostrich cannot have been lost on Job (and his wife), who practiced preemptive sacrifices just in case his children sinned.[18]

---

18. Ellen F. Davis, *Getting Involved with God: Rediscovering the Old Testament* (Boston: Cowley, 2001), 137–38.

Job's wife, more than even Job himself, undergoes the tremendously vulnerable and brave act of having more children. Job's wife knows that she cannot protect her children from danger any more than she could save her previous children. She may also have to mourn them. Just as God practices productivity and fertility that makes no sense, like watering the wastelands (38:27), Job's wife risks having more children after all her previous children have been killed, even though she could have controlled and limited her amount of heartache.[19] After all of her suffering, Job's wife chooses to "risk delight."[20] In so doing, for the second time in the book of Job, she emulates God more closely than any other figure in the text.

Conclusion

Job's wife has undergone drastically divergent treatments in the history of interpretation. She has been understood as the helpmate of the devil who incites her husband to curse God. As Dinah, however, she is also an expert in dealing with trauma who discerns a path forward that seeks to minimize her husband's suffering at the same time that it allows him to continue to be faithful to God. Job recognizes that her advice comes from her past trauma and accordingly chooses a different path. But their disagreement does not prevent their reunion after a period of suffering to risk restarting their family together. Though mentioned only briefly in the text, Job's wife echoes God when she first speaks and ultimately co-creates a new reality with him, emulating God's wild (re)productivity. Even without a large speaking role, her presence, actions, and words are critically important to the book of Job.

---

19. See b. Sotah 12b for the tale of Amram and Yocheved divorcing to prevent the heartbreak of having to expose male children, but Miriam the prophet convincing them to remarry and risk childbirth because God's mission may be at stake.

20. Jack Gilbert, "A Brief for the Defense," in *Refusing Heaven: Poems* (New York: Knopf, 2005), 1.

Implications for Ministry

How often are the folks who have "been through a lot" ignored or shunned because of their seemingly outrageous behavior or unorthodox perspectives? Trauma survivors can be intimidating, because frequently the veneer of polite society that presumes social safety is inaccessible to them/us. It is difficult to presume the world is a safe and gentle place when we know better. All too often, survivors are written off because they are either too jaded or too insistent on overcoming adversity and challenge. Dinah may be both too jaded and too insistent on practicing hope, maybe at the same time.

When Job is in the thick of his life falling apart, after their children have died, Dinah advises him to cling to his integrity, bless God, and cease his struggle and suffering. But Job recognizes the deep anguish and retraumatization from which Dinah spoke to him. Job chooses to remind Dinah, and perhaps himself, that humans receive good and ill, and both are a part of life. Ultimately, Dinah embraces the beauty among the heartbreak and joins Job in having ten more children, giving their daughters sensual names—"Cooing Dove," "Cinnamon," and "Jar of Eyeliner." Dinah risks delight and points toward finding beauty in everyday wonders.

Trauma survivors speak wisdom, if only we will listen. But, like Job, we also need to be sensitive to when survivors speak out of woundedness and when they speak out of their healing. My dear friend is a survivor of serial spiritual abuse. And she will be the first to recognize that sometimes when she speaks about churches, she voices more frustration and disillusionment than anything else. But there is no one better at identifying the roots of narcissism in leadership and abdication of the responsibilities of congregations to insist on following God rather than charismatic leaders. We ignore my friend's hard-fought wisdom at our peril. We ignore Dinah's insistence on creating beauty from ashes at our peril. Who are the wise ones among you who have experienced enough trauma and healing to know how to save others? Or, as a survivor, how are you speaking out of healing instead of speaking out of hurt? Dinah gives us a gift in demonstrating both despair and hope, and finishing with the latter.

6

SURVIVORS FIGHTING FOR JUSTICE

Scripture: Genesis 38

> *And Judah recognized them, and said, "She is more righteous than I, since I did not give her to my son Shelah."*
>
> —Genesis 38:26

THE STORY OF Judah and Tamar in Genesis 38 offers a fascinating glimpse at sexual and familial mores from an early period of Hebrew-Canaanite interactions. While focusing on the ancestors of Judah's royal family, the text displays a deep continuity with the Joseph novella, in the middle of which it is located. The use of multiple characters in Genesis 38, many of whom show up only to die a few verses later, serves to reinforce the focus on Judah and Tamar, who together found the family out of which the Davidic dynasty will spring. I argue that the two main characters, Tamar and Judah, are not judged as moral equals in the text. Judah proclaims the truth that Tamar the Canaanite is more righteous than he is. So, while the text itself seems concerned with the rise of the royal family of Judah, and it is surrounded by a narrative of the rise of the house of Joseph (to be addressed in the next chapter), the moral center of the narrative is Tamar using deception to take what she is owed after her traumatic mistreatment. Tamar's ruse of pretending to be a sex worker in order to lure her father-in-law to impregnate her is explicitly framed as restorative justice. Tamar, after years of being sexually neglected and deprived by her partners, takes matters into her own hands and acquires reproductive sex for herself.

Characters

Literarily, Genesis 38 is focused on introducing characters who will be important for the rest of the Bible's narrative. So, we must pay attention to the key (human) actors in the text. Judah is frequently, and I would argue erroneously, presented as the main character. He has left his brothers and gone down to live with the Canaanites. His good friend Hirah, who plays an important role in the story, is at the very least non-Israelite. His wife, Bathshua, is the daughter of a Canaanite. Judah undergoes a great change in the story as he transitions from a jealous father protecting his last son to a father-in-law who recognizes that Tamar's claim on his family is more righteous than his desire to protect them from her.

About Bathshua we know relatively little from the biblical text. She was Canaanite and gave birth to three sons, Er, Onan, and Shelah, before she died. The text says that Judah saw her and then married/took her, so we know that she lived at least a semipublic life such that Judah was able to see her before they were married. Contrary to his sons, each of Judah's sexual encounters with Bathshua leads to procreation.[1] After her death, Judah seeks sexual companionship with a woman whom he thought was a sex worker.

Hirah of Adullam comes from a royal city of the Canaanites.[2] That he is Judah's friend is reiterated in the text (Gen 38:12, 20). He also seems to act as a servant-agent when Judah sends him to pay off the supposed sex worker with whom he left his identifying materials. It is not explicit in the text, but interpreters have long suggested that Hirah was the friend who told Tamar that her father-in-law was on the move and where he could be found (38:13). If this was the case, Hirah took steps to restore to Tamar what she had been prevented from claiming.

---

1. Alexander Abasili, "Seeing Tamar through the Prism of an African Woman: A Contextual Reading of Genesis 38," *OTE* 24, no. 3 (2001): 557.
2. Sarna, *Genesis*, 265.

Er was Bathshua and Judah's first son. His name probably means something like "vigilant" (Gen. Rab. 85:4), but note the wordplay that Er (עֵר) was evil (רַע) in the sight of the Lord (Gen 38:7). The rabbis (b. Yevam. 34b and Rashi on 38:7) suppose that Er practiced abusive sex against/with Tamar.

Onan rightfully receives much of the social opprobrium when this passage is discussed. His name probably meant "vigorous" but came to be associated with "grief" (Gen. Rab. 85:4). Some combination of his refusing to raise up children for his brother and his spilling his seed on the ground (Gen 38:9) leads to his execution by the divine. Having repeated sexual access to Tamar but refusing to produce a child for her flies in the face of concept of *yibbum* (a brother-in-law providing heirs).[3] By precluding reproduction, Onan transfers sex with his deceased brother's wife from the meritorious provision of an heir to the forbidden act of sex with a prohibited partner.[4]

Shelah was Bathshua's and Judah's youngest son. His name probably means something like "taken out," but the root can also mean "be negligent" (see 2 Kgs 4:28; 2 Chr 29:11), a possible play on Judah being negligent in giving Shelah to Tamar. By refusing to give him to her, Judah forbids him from fulfilling the role of a *yavam*, or heir provider, to his sister-in-law.

Tamar's name means "date palm." Judah secures her for his first son, Er (Gen 38:6). After Er's and Onan's deaths, however, Judah sends her home to her father's house to await sexual provision from Shelah. Seeing that that is not going to happen, "after a long time" (vv. 12, 14), she takes matters into her own hands. Tamar takes off her mourning garments, wears a disguising veil, and uses Judah's sexuality to secure

---

3. Claus Westermann, *Genesis 37–50: A Commentary*, trans. John Scullion (Minneapolis: Augsburg, 1986), 52.

4. Sarna, *Genesis*, 267. Westermann goes further to state that Onan's case is the cultural memory that provokes Lev 20:21, which seems to prohibit the practice of *yavam* entirely (*Genesis 37–50*, 52).

for herself offspring. She becomes the progenitrix of the royal family in Judah.

Susan Niditch notes that matriarchs in the Hebrew Bible usually enact and reinforce certain themes: (1) the private/nonpublic role of wife and mother, (2) the role of linking men through marriage alliances, and (3) the powerlessness of women who fail to fulfill their roles as wife and/or mother.[5] Tamar seems to be an exception to the rule. She acts at the crossroads and at her own execution to publicly claim her position in Judah's family. Tamar's family is not introduced, and Judah seems uninterested in an alliance with them. Rather, Judah seems eager to send Tamar back to her father's house after Onan's death and eager to execute her at her father's house when he hears reports of her sexual actions. Finally, Tamar is anything but powerless as she acts to claim what Judah's family owes her through her deception of the patriarch.

A strong case can be made for Tamar being the central figure of this story rather than Judah. Tamar's story is utterly unique: she is presented as an unmarried, presumable virgin, then a wife, a widow, a wife again, and a widow again. As she was returned to her father's house, the rabbis strongly suggest that neither of her marriages was fully consummated, so she remained at least somewhat virginal. It was only in setting aside her propriety to "play the whore" that she at last had reproductive sexual intercourse.[6] As long as she remained a wife/widow/virgin, she was denied a family. But it was her "whoredom" that led to not only progeny but also the intentionally misleading sex act that led to Judah to declare her righteous.

Telling the Story Again

The story of Tamar is founded on the duty of a husband's family to take care of a wife who becomes a childless widow. Tamar was married

---

5. Niditch, "Genesis," 33.

6. Eve Rebecca Parker, "The Virgin and the Whore—An Interreligious Challenge for Our Times," *The Ecumenical Review* 71, no. 5 (2019): 694.

to Judah's son Er. When Er was killed by God and died childless, Tamar was married to Er's brother Onan. When Onan was smitten by God for mistreatment of Tamar, Judah returned Tamar to her parents' home rather than give her the husband—and reproductive sex—she was owed.

The rabbis argue that Tamar was a serially dehumanized sexual plaything for her first two husbands, Judah's sons Er and Onan: something they enjoyed playing with but never actually brought to satisfactory climax. While Er's abuse is implicit, Onan's cynical abuse of Tamar for nonreproductive sexual actions is explicit. Most commentors and translators assume that Onan's semen was what was "on the ground" (Gen 38:9), though the wording of the passage leaves open the possibility that it was not "seed" but "his brother's wife" who is the direct object of the verb. Read this way, Onan traumatically "destroyed" or "spoiled" Tamar on/facing the ground in nonreproductive sexual activity. The passage pictures Onan violently anally raping Tamar. These actions make God shake with anger (understanding *yera* as "to shake/quiver"), and so Onan is *also* killed. This passage, coupled with the later commandment that Israelite men not deprive their wives of pleasure (Exod 21:10), forms the scriptural basis of a positive responsibility to ensure sexual pleasure for—and proscribe sexual violence against—wives.

The rabbis were particularly interested in the "also" in Genesis 38:10 and retroactively applied Onan's evil to Er. If what Onan *did* was evil, Er must have performed that same activity habitually, because Er *was* evil in God's sight (38:7). Er exclusively practiced "unnatural intercourse" with Tamar, despite her protestations, that allowed Er to climax but did not risk impregnating Tamar. Er enjoyed Tamar's beautiful, nubile form and did not wish for her body to be changed by childbirth (b. Yevam. 34b). The rabbis understood that God killed Tamar's first two husbands because of repeated marital anal rape and that even after these men had their way with her, she was still a vaginal virgin. After the death of his two sons, Judah sent Tamar back to her father's house as both a widow and a "pure" virgin (b. Sotah 10a). Eve

Rebecca Parker notes that Tamar's journey takes her "from virgin, to wife, to widow, to betrothed, to prostitute, to righteous," and Tamar is simultaneously a virgin while also "playing the whore."[7]

After the death of his two eldest sons, Judah is not interested in chancing the marriage of his youngest, Selah, to Tamar, seeing her as the causative agent in the deaths of his sons. Sitting in her father's home, Tamar is increasingly aware that she was an *agunah*, or a chained woman.[8] Perpetually betrothed to a grown man who would never be her husband, Tamar's sexuality was controlled by Judah, who denied her reproductive sexuality every bit as much, though less cruelly, as Er and Onan had years before. After Judah's Canaanite wife dies, an unnamed informer (could it be a well-intentioned Hirah the Adullamite?) sends word that Judah is no longer mourning and is on his way to Timnah.

Tamar decides to act. Her sexuality is owned by men who will neither satisfy her nor release her to another. The virginal rape survivor commits to a performance of female sexuality different from any she has practiced to that point. The rabbis read 38:14 as central to Tamar's performance: "So she removed from herself her widow's garments and covered with a garment, and wrapped herself, and sat" (my translation). Rashi and Genesis Rabbah follow the tradition that Tamar put on a veil to disguise herself from her father-in-law (Gen. Rab. 85:8).

But Rashi also refers to a talmudic tradition that takes a different tack. Understanding that women seeking to solicit money for sex rarely cover their faces but rather display themselves brazenly, the talmudic author reasons that verse 14 must not be saying that Tamar *put on* additional covering to attract Judah. The writer understands the second two verbs as a phrase describing Tamar's modesty as a widow,

---

7. Parker, "Virgin and the Whore," 695.

8. A woman who is trapped in an engagement or marriage to someone who is absent and will not fulfill marital responsibilities is considered an *agunah*. Typically, these are women whose husbands have left without granting them a divorce *get*, who are then unable to remarry.

and even before that as a married woman in the presence of her father-in-law. The Talmud argues that Tamar "took off her widow's garments [that is:] putting on a veil and wrapping herself up—and sat down." Out of modesty, Tamar had always covered her face and concealed her form in Judah's presence, even during her marriages to Er and Onan. So when she sat in his path, he beheld her full face for the first time (b. Sotah 10b). This midrash underscores the radicality of Tamar's disguise: the modest virgin performed sexually available and immodest femininity to have righteous sexual intercourse for the first time with a man to whom she was not married but who nevertheless owned her sexuality. To reenforce the point, the rabbis understand that Tamar planned and executed the seduction at "the entrance to Enaim," possibly rendered as the "the opening of the eyes" (Gen. Rab. 85:7; b. Sotah 10a). Tamar has opened her eyes, face, and entire body to Judah, but Judah is unable to recognize his unveiled daughter-in-law.[9]

Before Judah can have intercourse with her, Tamar demands terms of payment. Judah did not provide a husband or return her dowry as she sat in her father's house, and so Tamar seeks to provide for herself a man, children, material provision, and safety all at once. Judah offers to send her a goat kid from his flocks, but Tamar asks for surety until he sends the animal: Judah's cylinder seal, the cord he wears it on, and his staff. The payment and surety agreed upon, Tamar instigates the kind of sex she desires for the first time in her life. Tamar has gained power through taking control of her sexuality and having a mutual conversation about what she and Judah want. In doing so, Tamar performs feminine self-ownership. Parker argues, "Tamar wears the veil of 'indecency' to shame the systems of oppression and be righteous before God."[10]

---

9. Rachel Adelman, "Seduction and Recognition in the Story of Judah and Tamar and the Book of Ruth," *NASHIM: A Journal of Jewish Women's Studies and Gender Issues* 23, no. 1 (2012): 93.

10. Parker, "Virgin and the Whore," 705.

We should note that Tamar's deception here differs strongly from that of Leah with Jacob. Jacob specified that he loved Rachel, came to terms with Laban to marry Rachel, had a ceremony for his wedding with Rachel, and then was surprised to find Leah in his bed by substitution of the intended partner for another without consent. Judah, on the other hand, made a deal to have sex with a person without attempting to specify who she was and then slept with the person with whom he made the agreement. Judah was surprised, to be sure, but he was not raped.

After her encounter with Judah, Tamar puts back on her widow's clothes and her characteristic feminine-gendered modesty (Gen 38:19). Even in defending her own life after she becomes pregnant and is charged with adultery against Judah's ownership of her sexuality, the rabbis notice that Tamar maintains modesty. She does not publicly accuse Judah. Instead, Tamar sends his seal, cord, and staff to him with the surprisingly gentle request not only to "please examine and see" (Gen 38:25) that he impregnated her but to truly recognize Tamar as a victim of sexual violence and maltreatment at the hands of Judah's family, and to recognize the children who would be burned within her as Judah's own (Gen. Rab. 85:11, b. Sotah 10b).

Judah recognizes his effects, and more importantly, recognizes Tamar fully, pronouncing her more righteous than himself. But Judah is never intimate with her again (Gen 38:26). Tamar, victimized by men who mistreated her and dismissed her own sexual agency, endures a final, lifelong neglect. She is in every sense still bound to the family of Judah and cannot have nonadulterous sex with anyone but Judah. Judah chooses for her to be perpetually chained to the family in a sexless relationship for the rest of her life.

Genesis Rabbah (85:9) neatly sums up what Tamar is left with after she returns Judah's identifying objects and is left without hope for a husband. Even after Tamar returns Judah's seal (*khotamet*), she retains in her womb kingship, as her descendant, King Jeconiah son of Jehoiakim, is described as "a signet ring [*khotam*] on My right hand"

(Jer 22:24). Even after Tamar returns Judah's cord, she retains descendants who will sit on the Sanhedrin, distinct among their community, like the special blue *tekelet* cord among the *tsitsit* (Num 15:38). And even after Tamar returns Judah's staff, she retains the seed of the eventual anointed king/messiah in her womb, as it is said, "The Lord will stretch forth from Zion your mighty staff" (Ps 110:2, my translation). Judah takes back his identifying objects and withholds all future sexual contact from Tamar. But the rabbis hold that Judah was unable to take back from her the royalty and holiness of their offspring.

For one, brief encounter, Tamar performed self-ownership and practiced her sexuality by her choice. But that encounter was a fleeting moment in an otherwise involuntary celibate life. In deciding not to touch her again, the text only specifies Judah's agency in making the decision. But when Tamar was able to make her own decisions, she was sexually active and intentional about getting what she wanted.

Even in Tamar's sad status of a perpetual *agunah*, the rabbis preserve a glimmer of sexual hope. Where "he did not know her again" seems to be the plain reading and the interpretation of Sifre Numbers (88), the Talmud sees the repetition of terms in *welo yasaf od ledatah* to indicate a double negative, for example, "he did not cease to know her" (b. Sotah 10b). Perhaps Tamar gained a husband, or at least a frequent sexual partner, after all.

Tamar gives birth to twin boys. Genesis Rabbah notes that these twins were superior in moral character to the twins of their great-grandmother. Whereas there were תוֹמִם (*towmim*, a deficient spelling) in Rebekah's womb (Gen 25:24), there were תְאוֹמִים (*teowmim*; adding the *alef* and *yod*) in Tamar's womb (38:27). The defective spelling of Rebekah's twins reflects the defective character of Esau and his violence and entrapment of people and animals. Perez and Zerah were both righteous, however, and therefore the correct spelling of "twins" reflects their correct behavior (Gen. Rab. 85:13). Tamar is put on the same level as the matriarchs and in fact excels them in having perfectly righteous children. Even Leah's Reuben dishonors his father, but Perez and Zerah are completely unlike their evil half-brothers and morally deficient uncles.

"She Is More Right than I"

The text is careful to point out that Judah is not at fault for having sex with his daughter-in-law, even as it does not shy away from presenting the problematic sexual union that results in the illustrious family. The text repeatedly states that Judah had no idea it was Tamar with whom he slept: "When Judah saw her, he took her for a sex worker, for she had her face covered" (Gen 38:15, my translation), and "he did not know that she was his daughter-in-law" (38:16). Ironically, Judah does not recognize his daughter-in-law as she sat at *petah enayim*, the "opening of eyes" (38:14).[11]

But if Judah was not at fault for being deceived into sleeping with his daughter-in-law, he was certainly still responsible for her situation as a woman trapped in a state of being a promised widow whose rightful sexual partner was being withheld from her. The relative power of Judah over Tamar, and even over his children, pervades the whole story. The text is clear that Judah had no plans to fulfill his responsibility to provide an heir for Tamar, Er, or Onan: "She saw that Shelah had grown up, but she had not been given to him" (38:14, my translation). This was a serious deprivation of rights to progeny. Not unlike Onan (and possibly Er), Judah intentionally used his male power as patriarch of the family to deny reproductive sexual intercourse to Tamar. She neither had a partner nor was free to find one for herself. Meanwhile, Judah visited a supposed sex worker, demonstrating that he, like Er and Onan, felt entitled to pleasurable, nonreproductive sexual encounters.[12]

The denial of procreative sexual interaction was not the only way in which Judah used his power to prevent Shelah and Tamar from

---

11. Aderman, "Seduction and Recognition," 93.

12. Chaya Greenberger, "Judah and Tamar: Self-Esteem Lost and (Partially) Redeemed," *JBQ* 48, no. 1 (2020): 29.

fulfilling their duties. When Tamar was found to be with child, Judah ordered that she be burned to death (38:24). This seems extreme, especially given that the later capital punishment for sexual crimes in Deuteronomy 22:21, 24 is death by stoning (though the method of execution for adultery in Deut 22:22 is not specified).[13] Nahum Sarna notes that burning of adulterers may have reflected contemporary Canaanite practice, but also that Nachmanides believed the brutality of the method of execution indicated Judah's elevated status and that a sexual offense against him (as the owner of Tamar's sexuality) was like an offense against a great king.[14] Pain and a horrific public display seems to have been the goal for Judah in disposing of his daughter-in-law, rather than a relatively quick death.

In response to these charges, and literally as she was being brought out to be burned alive, Tamar produced Judah's seal, cord, and staff and asked that Judah "please examine and see" (Gen 38:25) the items that proved that he had fathered her children. This was the crucial moment of accountability in which Judah could have gotten rid of an annoying relation just as he had years earlier with Joseph. In that earlier occasion, the brothers had asked Jacob to "please examine it to see" (Gen 37:32) the torn and bloodied special garment that Jacob had given to Joseph. Tamar gave Judah an opportunity to redeem himself, at least partially, by recognizing his personal objects and in the process sparing her from death. At the production of these identifying objects, Judah concluded, "She is more righteous than I!" (Gen 38:26) because he had not given his son Shelah to her.

The rabbis (b. Sotah 10b) see Judah's confessional response to Tamar's plea to "please examine and see" as a turning point in his moral arc. Tamar helped Judah to recognize—and tricked him into performing—his responsibility to preserve the lives (and names) of his family. Westermann notes that Tamar's "conduct was justified by

---

13. Westermann, *Genesis 37–50*, 54.
14. Sarna, *Genesis*, 269.

[Judah's] own injustice."[15] He had purposely prevented the fulfillment of his family's responsibility to Er, Onan, and Tamar to provide children. Because of his sinful use of power to deny Tamar offspring, her deceptive acquisition of Judah's sexuality was retroactively pronounced to be more righteous than his denial of hers.

Context and Continuity: Looking Forward

The details of the story of Judah and Tamar may at first glance seem to be merely an interruption of the Joseph novella. The rabbis have long held that the stories of Tamar and Mrs. Potiphar are linked purposefully. Rabbi Samuel Bar Nachman argues that the stories were held together to show that just as the illicit sex between Judah and Tamar "accomplished the purposes of Heaven," so too did the false accusation of illicit sex levied by Mrs. Potiphar against Joseph that we will examine next occur for heaven's sake (Gen. Rab. 85:2). On the other hand, the story of Judah and Tamar may have been inserted here as a literary device to heighten tension as the reader/hearer wonders what will happen to Joseph, who has just been sold into slavery.[16] However, other readers will see parallel accounts of marginal figures standing up for their own rights and marshaling evidence to their defense. In any case, the stories of Judah and Tamar on the one hand and Joseph and Mrs. Potiphar on the other share a deep thematic continuity.

The most obvious link between the two chapters and two stories is the allegations and practices of problematic sex. There are three instances in just these two chapters. The first is when Onan, Judah's second son, uses some kind of unauthorized sexual practice to prevent himself from impregnating Tamar and fulfilling his duty as a *yavam* (lit. "begetter"; Deut 25:7) to a childless widow (Gen 38:9).[17] The second instance is when Judah accuses Tamar of illegal sex because she

---

15. Westermann, *Genesis 37–50*, 55.
16. Sarna, *Genesis*, 263.
17. Westermann, *Genesis 37–50*, 48.

has been impregnated by someone other than Shelah, her next brother-in-law, who owns her sexuality (38:24–26). Judah, of course, is the father of Tamar's children because he slept with her, thinking she was an anonymous woman working as a sex worker rather than his daughter-in-law with a claim on his family for offspring. The third instance of allegations of impermissible sex is when Mrs. Potiphar alleges that Joseph tried to rape her (39:13–18).

In and amid these stories of contested recounting of sexual activity in Genesis 38–39, personal items are used to prove righteousness, in the case of Tamar (seal, cord, and staff), and as a false proof of guilt, in the case of Joseph (torn garment). In both the narratives of Judah/Tamar and Mrs. Potiphar/Joseph, there is an intersectional dynamic of power and ethnicity at play. Judah, as a Hebrew, seems to have had power to order an execution, and a particularly violent one (38:24), of a Canaanite in an area populated by mainly Canaanites prior to the conquest(s) of the Land. Mrs. Potiphar, as an Egyptian and the wife of a courtier of Pharaoh (39:1), would have had nearly unlimited power over a Hebrew slave such as Joseph.

The final linkage between the chapters is the notions of Judah's ascendency. The interlude of chapter 38 provides the narrative of the birth of David's ancestors from Judah. Even in the Joseph novella, however, Judah plays a strong role as he comes up with the plan to sell Joseph (37:26), becomes a leader in dealing with the silver cup (44:14–34), and finally leads the immigration project into Egypt (46:28).[18] While the narrative's focal shifts from Joseph to Judah and then back to Joseph may feel drastic, there are strong thematic linkages among these chapters.

Beyond shared thematic elements, the linguistic similarities between chapter 38 and its surroundings are strong as well. The shared language intentionally sets the scene and foreshadows the traumatic experiences in the connected stories. The root *olah* ("to ascend")

---

18. Sarna, *Genesis*, 264.

plays a vital role as Joseph is "taken up" out of the pit by Midianites (37:28), Judah "went up" to celebrate and shear his sheep (38:12–13), the cupbearer dreams of vines that "shot up" (40:10), both cows and corn "came up" out of the Nile (41:2, 3, 5, 18–19, 22, 27), and most poignantly Joseph speaks with his brothers about "going up" to their father (44:17, 24, 33).

The positional language also flows the other way. The root *yered* ("to descend") is used to describe how the Ishmaelites are "going down" to Egypt (37:25), that Jacob will "go down" to his grave in mourning for Joseph (37:35), that Judah "went down" from his brothers to his friend Hirah (38:1), and how Joseph is "taken down" to Egypt (39:1).[19] Rashi notes that rather than just a geographic descent, Judah's relationship with his brothers had deteriorated such that they "demoted him" *shhoridoho* from his high position (Tanhuma Buber, Vayeshev 8). Rashi holds that Judah then turned aside *from his brothers / meet ahayv* (Gen 38:1) as a response to his loss of esteem in their eyes. The Tamar and Judah story, far from being an irrelevant insertion, becomes the dramatic centerpiece in an ongoing family crisis, in which the descents of Jacob, Joseph, and Judah are turned around from their collective descents to rise again.[20]

Goats (*izim*) play important plot devices, in addition to repeated vocabulary, linking the Judah interlude with the Joseph novella. It is a hairy goat that the brothers use to convince their poor father that Joseph has been killed, while a kid from the flock is the price that Judah promises Tamar for sleeping with her. Remember, Rebekah's and Jacob's deception of Isaac was only possible because of a goat kid. The goat in these stories is an instrument of deception or part of an attempt to mislead.

In a section of the Bible that involves so much deception and misleading, the verb *nakar* ("to discern/recognize") plays a remarkable role as Jacob is asked to "discern" whether the torn and bloodied coat

---

19. Sarna, *Genesis*, 263.
20. Greenberger, "Judah and Tamar," 23.

is that of Joseph (Gen 37:32–33) and then as Tamar asks Judah to "discern" whose staff, seal, and cord she possesses (39:25–26). The reader/hearer is called on to discern, in the "fuzzy, messy and icky," who is being misled or abused and who is righteous, if anyone.[21] The language used throughout this section points to important continuity rather than a disjuncture between chapter 38 and its surroundings.

In addition to the common language, clothing-as-evidence, and confusion about sexual rights with a foreigners, there is a strong continuity of focusing on moral obligation to work justice for victims of sexual abuse. A non-Israelite woman demands and seizes sex that she is owed and is judged righteous. An Israelite man declines sex that would have been adulterous and is prosecuted for his presumed guilt but is later freed and acquitted by God and Pharoah. The author of Genesis is providing opportunity for commenting on deception, sexuality, power, ethnicity, and gender.

Conclusion

Phyllis Trible notes that in the Tamar and Judah story, the reader witnesses "women working out their own salvation with fear and trembling, for it is God who works in them."[22] Tamar is judged by the narrative, and by Judah himself, as the most righteous character. She tricked him into sex with his own daughter-in-law, but only after he failed the most basic provision for his familial responsibilities. Judah ordered Onan to provide an heir for his brother Er, but he was unwilling to do it. God smote Onan. When Judah refused to do what was in his power to produce an heir for Er, Onan, and Tamar, he somehow escaped punishment but not self-censure. Judah's own pronouncement that Tamar was more righteous than he was shows that even at the founding of the tribe of Judah, might does not make right. Women's

---

21. Graybill, *Texts after Terror*, 40.

22. Phyllis Trible, *God and the Rhetoric of Sexuality* (Philadelphia: Fortress, 1979), 196.

sexuality may be controlled by men, but men disregard their responsibilities to women at their peril. Sadly, the mistreatment of women by men in the royal line of Judah will continue in the lives of David and his children. Judah is, of course, married to Bathshua, and it is her death that leads him to go out with his friend and seek sexual companionship (Gen 38:12). Interestingly, "Bathshua" (38:12) is the form that most Hebrew manuscripts use for Bathsheba, David's wife, in 1 Chronicles 3:5.[23] Tamar is a name associated in the Bible only with the royal family in Judah.[24] The other Tamar in the Bible appears in the story of her rape by her half-brother. The sexual abuse experienced by this Tamar is meant to be recognized as a call forward/callback to the loathsome experience of women in Judah's royal family. Thankfully, women named Tamar, however, always receive their vindication.

Implications for Ministry

Parker points out that Walter Brueggemann once famously noted of the Tamar narrative that "it is difficult to know in what context it may be of value for theological exposition."[25] But this text is "passionately theological, as it brings to light a woman's lived faith journey embedded within a patriarchal world that is entrenched within an ideology that seeks to control her body."[26] Tamar is abused, traumatized, and neglected by Judah and his sons. Yet, Tamar chooses to set aside her characteristic modesty to reinvent herself as a woman who negotiates with men on an equal footing to decide what she will do with her sexuality. Tamar's open face is a disguise to the man who has only seen

---

23. Sarna, *Genesis*, 265.

24. Tamar is a daughter of David (see 2 Sam 13). Tamar bat David's brother, Absalom, named his own daughter after his sister (2 Sam 14:27; see Sarna, *Genesis*, 266).

25. Walter Brueggemann, *Genesis* (Atlanta: John Knox, 1982), 308. It must be noted that this work was written forty years ago and that much has changed since.

26. Parker, "Virgin and the Whore," 701.

her performing modest femininity in the tents of his sons. Tamar then returns to her modesty, even in the face of judicial murder. Tamar knows who she is and lives her commitments.

Tamar could have grown old in her father's house, presumably with a stipend from Judah's family for maintenance. But Tamar wanted what she was due. Tamar the Canaanite outwitted her father-in-law and appealed to his sense of righteousness to recognize that not only had he sinned in depriving Tamar of a sexual partner to meet her demands but that she had been righteous in taking what she was owed.

After trauma, and most especially trauma at the hands of multiple sexual partners, how do we support healthy and righteous sexuality? Tamar looked and saw that Shelah had grown, and she was being deprived. When victims look and see that the time is right to practice their righteous sexuality after abuse, we can be like Judah and ignore, deprive, or postpone. Or, we can be like Hirah and trust, support, and aid victims who are healed enough to find an appropriate mate. Keeping someone as an *agunah*, or chained to an abusive or nonexistent relationship, is not the fullness that God intends for survivors.

Tamar knew the righteousness of her actions even before Judah pronounced them. Tamar, even more than the matriarchs, gave birth to righteous sons. One midrash says that Tamar was only noticed to be pregnant at the relatively early date of three months (Gen 38:24) because she would walk around patting her belly and proclaiming, "I am pregnant with kings and redeemers" (Gen. Rab. 85:10). Tamar was not ashamed to have reclaimed her sexuality from previous husbands who degraded her and ignored her desires. Er, Onan, and even Judah denied Tamar healthy, holy sex. Judah simply wanted her to go away. But Tamar survived abuse, claimed—even if only briefly—ownership of her body and sexuality, and became the mother of kings, redeemers, and messiah(s). Who in your life needs the permission of Tamar to reclaim their sexuality and live as a survivor of abuse and neglect that will no longer define them?

7

PATHWAYS TO RESISTANCE AND FREEDOM

Scripture: Genesis 39

> *Now it happened one day that he went into the house to do his work, and none of the people of the household was there inside. So she grabbed him by his garment, saying, "Sleep with me!" But he left his garment in her hand and fled, and went outside.*
>
> —Genesis 39:11–12

THE STORY OF Joseph and his harassment and assault at the hands of Potiphar's wife is an understudied resource for thinking about sexual violence committed by women against men. In order to think through how such crimes might be understood and how restitution might be made to the victims by the perpetrators, I will conduct a close reading of the biblical text, highlighting issues of how irresponsibility, racism, and dehumanization lead to the victimization of an enslaved foreigner in Potiphar's house. Joseph's story is particularly important as it will allow us to think through the intersectional nature of traumatizing violence. I will then try to explore how some interpretative communities have expressed discomfort with the idea of a male victim of female sexual violence. Finally, I will provide hypothetical suggestions for how a repentant Potiphar and wife could work toward healing for Joseph and for themselves.

A Biblical Case Study

The textual witness of the encounter between the wife of Potiphar (hereafter "Mrs. Potiphar" or "Zuleika," the name used in later Jewish and Islamic interpretation) and Joseph is full of important details that paint a picture of a situation of ongoing domestic sexual terrorism that ends with false accusation and imprisonment of the victim and uncertainty about the fate of the abuser and accuser.[1]

After Potiphar, captain of Pharaoh's guards, buys Joseph, who was sold into slavery by his brothers, he is immediately set to work in the home of Potiphar, where he also resides (Gen 39:2). Enslaved Asians seemed to have been favored for household activities in Egyptian homes, whereas enslaved Egyptians and other Africans were usually confined to the fields for work and outbuildings for residence.[2] One may hazard a guess whether the lighter-complexioned Asians were forced to serve in Egyptian homes because they were more readily distinguishable as servants from darker-skinned Egyptian guests and residents. Or there may have been a sort of racialized assumptions about Asiatic suitability for administrative tasks. In any case, Joseph is living in relatively close quarters with Potiphar in his home.

In this context of household interaction, Potiphar observes that everything Joseph does meets with success. Potiphar first makes Joseph his personal servant and then places Joseph in charge of his entire household. Eventually, Potiphar places everything he owns, literally, in Joseph's hands (39:4, 6). Potiphar then seems to back off from interacting with his household and property, *knowing* only the bread he eats. I argue that the hearers/readers are to understand that this means that Potiphar did not "know" his wife (see Gen 4:1, 17, 25). He is, after all, a *saris*, or eunuch (39:1).

Immediately after this self-isolating of Potiphar, the text notes that Joseph was attractive. But the phrase used, *yosef yefeh toar wipeh*

---

1. Michael Johnson, "Domestic Violence: It's Not about Gender—Or Is It?," *Journal of Marriage and Family* 67, no. 5 (2005): 1127.

2. Papyri records (Brooklyn 35.1446) of Egyptian households' slaves and their occupations demonstrate superiority in household status of Asian slaves who were given administrative tasks, with Egyptian slaves being relegated to the more physically demanding field tasks (Sarna, *Genesis*, 271).

mareh, is not used for any other male person in the biblical text. The closest usage is in fact the description of Joseph's mother, Rachel, when Jacob seeks to marry her (29:17). The rabbis will make much of the feminized description of Joseph's attractiveness.

In the meantime, after unnamed events pass (39:7), Potiphar's wife directs her eyes toward Joseph and tells him in completely unadorned language to lie with her. Joseph refuses at once, but does so in a strange way: by noting his authority in Potiphar's neglected house. Joseph charges Mrs. Potiphar to notice that Potiphar does not know/"know" anything/anyone in the household, and Joseph's master—Potiphar is not, tellingly, referred to as Zuleika's husband—has placed everything he owned into Joseph's hands (v. 8). Joseph continues that there is no one greater in the household than himself (v. 9). Finally, Joseph notes that Potiphar has withheld not the least speck of anything from Joseph except Zuleika herself. Up until this point, Joseph may be praising himself as a worthy sexual match for Mrs. Potiphar by noting his position in the household and that Potiphar is not greater than him. Eventually, however, Joseph notes that their sexual intimacy is forbidden. Then Joseph invokes God to say that he will not do this great sin (v. 9).

Zuleika does not accept Joseph's refusal. On the contrary, she orders him to have sex with her. Joseph does not listen to her, does not lie with her, and even seeks not to be in her presence (Gen 39:10). Mrs. Potiphar then constructs a trap. One day, when Joseph goes into the house to do his work—has Joseph moved out of the house to sleep among the field slaves for relief from his sexual predator?—none of the other people who are a part of the large household of Pharaoh's captain of the guard are there (v. 11). They have doubtless been sent away for the trap. Zuleika catches Joseph by his "garment." Normal Egyptian attire for men, especially servants, was only a short men's skirt, called a *shendyt*. Mrs. Potiphar grabs Joseph over either his groin or his buttocks and once more commands him to lie with her. Joseph leaves the garment in her hand and runs away (naked), and the text notes that he left the entire household (v. 12).

Mrs. Potiphar immediately calls out to the household staff, who are, presumably, standing by and waiting to be called back after Mrs. Potiphar told them to leave the house. She hastily assembles her household and asserts that her husband brought in a different-race, foreign slave to *letsakheq* with "us" (v. 14). The verb in this sentence should probably be understood as "sexually molest" or "fondle," as in Genesis 26:8; 21:9; Exodus 32:6. Zuleika displays Joseph's *shendyt* to them and says that it was only her screaming that caused the attempted rapist to run away, leaving his garment. So, to be clear, after a daily routine of sexually harassing Joseph and trying to force him to have sex with her, Zuleika has engineered a trap, grabbed Joseph's genitals, torn off his one item of clothing, and caused him to flee. After all this, Mrs. Potiphar tells the assembled household that Potiphar brought Joseph, the foreign, racially different slave, to sexually molest an unspecified target group. After Joseph's master—again, not *her husband*—comes home, she tells him the same story, changing only her accusation that Potiphar brought the Hebrew slave to molest specifically *her alone* (v. 17). Potiphar is furious and throws Joseph in prison.

This is a shockingly graphic situation of how domestic sexual predation is shaped by issues of race, national origin, gender, and above all power. Foremost of the lingering questions this text raises are, first, after what events does Potiphar's wife look at Joseph with desire (v. 7)? Further, many, especially male, interpreters ask why Joseph, a man in the prime of life, refused to acquiesce to Mrs. Potiphar's demands, especially when she had at least as much interest in keeping them secret as he did. Last, when Mrs. Potiphar complained to the people of the household that Joseph has been brought to "make sport of us," who is "us," and why did she change her analysis of the target of mockery when speaking to her husband? But before exploring those questions, the Joseph and Mrs. Potiphar story must be contextualized in the surrounding narrative.

Ethnicity and Power

First, we must discuss the role of ethnicity and power in the Joseph and Zuleika story, especially in comparison to Tamar and Judah. In both stories, a non-Israelite woman attempts to seize the sexual initiative from an Israelite man. Tamar was a Canaanite daughter in the house of Judah—she was, in fact, sent back to the house of her parents before she literally became the parent of the majority of Judah's living offspring. She was able to outfox her father-in-law, a powerful man both within his clan (Gen 37:26–27) and among the Canaanites generally (38:1–2). In so doing, she displaced Bathshua and became essentially *the* mother of the tribe of Judah, and the royal line was counted through her son, Perez.

Zuleika, on the other hand, attempted to use Joseph, an enslaved Israelite foreigner in Egypt, for sexual enjoyment. The Genesis account records later that Egyptians generally held that Asian shepherds, like Joseph, were disgusting and did not associate with them if possible (46:34). Most slaves would have had almost no power, and an Asian shepherd like Joseph would have been especially despised. But as already noted above, Joseph was in the extraordinary position of essentially running Potiphar's household. We must wonder whether, when everything was put into Joseph's care, Zuleika also felt "handed over" in some way? Mrs. Potiphar was the only thing/person that/who had been withheld from Joseph by an otherwise disinterested husband. Zuleika's attraction to Joseph, across deep divides of ethnicity, power, and background, merits further, intersectional attention.

Interpreting Egyptian Women's Incredulity at Trans-class Attraction

The sages are fascinated with the class distinction between a predatory Egyptian woman, whose husband serves in Pharaoh's court, and a foreign slave. What could she have been thinking to be attracted to and then shame herself by repeated attempts to convince Joseph to have sex with her? The rabbis place their disbelief in the mouths of the other high-born Egyptian women, who are incredulous about how Potiphar's wife can be attracted to a slave from a particularly detestable background (Gen 46:34). To satisfy curiosity about a noblewoman becoming infatuated with her husband's slave, the rabbis envision Zuleika in ongoing conversation about race and class with the women of Pharaoh's court. When Mrs. Potiphar assembles the servants to falsely accuse Joseph, why does she say that Joseph was brought to make sport of "*us*" (39:14) and later say to her husband that he made sport of just her (39:17)? From this verse, the notion of a group of women who fell victim to Joseph's charms sprung into the minds of exegetes and commenters. One of the first explanations comes from Midrash Tanhuma:

> *No one may find a person of greater fidelity than Joseph, of while he was in Egypt, of whom it is written,* whose flesh is the flesh of donkeys *[they are very sexual] (Ezek. 23:20) and he was 17 years old; but he did not commit adultery. . . . The Rabbis of Blessed Memory said: Once the Egyptian women gathered and went to behold Joseph's beauty. What did the wife of Potiphar do? She took etrogs and gave them to each of them and gave each a knife and the called to Joseph and caused him to stand in front of them. When they beheld how handsome he was, they cut their hands. She said to them: If you do this after one moment, I who see at all moments, how much more so? Every day she tried to entice him with words, but he overcame his desires. How do we know this? From what we read next:* And after these things the wife of the master set her eyes upon him. *(Gen 39:7). (Midrash Tanhuma on Gen 39:7)*

The Egyptian women, who have beheld Joseph's beauty for just a moment, are so distracted from their tasks of peeling etrogs that they all accidentally slice their hands instead of the fruit. Mrs. Potiphar is able to use their wounds as witness against the other women that she is not mad or silly for desiring her servant. Thus, Mrs. Potiphar is no longer suffering her attraction to Joseph alone, but she now has a group of women who can attest to Joseph's devastating good looks and that harm that can come from them.

This theme of Zuleika relieving her social stigma for being attracted to a foreign slave by letting the other Egyptian women witness the attractiveness of Joseph is again picked up in Midrash Ha-Gadol:[3]

> *She put the righteous one [Joseph] in the mouths of all of them. They [the rabbis] said: When the queens and noble women returned from worshipping idols, they went to visit her [Mrs. Potiphar]. They said to her: Why do you look so bad? Have you perhaps been taken with that servant of yours? Then she gave them bread and meat and knives and brought Joseph in and caused him to stand before them. And when they lifted their eyes to Joseph, they cut their hands while eating. She said to them: If you, before whom he stood for just a moment were not able to endure, how much less able am I who see him every day? They said to her: You have no remedy but to tell his master to lock him up in prison and he will be completely yours. She said to them: If I am the only one to speak against him to my husband, he will not believe me. But if each of you tells her husband, "Joseph seized me," then I will tell my husband that Joseph seized me as well and he will put him in prison. (Midrash Ha-Gadol on Gen 39:7)*

From the opening sentence, Zuleika has attempted to give the other high-born Egyptian women the same hunger for Joseph's beautiful, foreign, enslaved body that burdens her daily. The Egyptian women, again, incredulously mock her for being so sexually obsessed with a foreign slave. After seeing Joseph, however, the other women are,

---

3. Solomon Fisch, "Midrash Ha-Gadol," *EncJud* 14:186.

again, instantly entranced. Mrs. Potiphar recruits the women to spread lies to all their husbands of Joseph's rapaciousness so that she will be believed when she tells Potiphar that Joseph attempted to rape her. The goal, in this instance, is not to preserve Zuleika's honor but to imprison Joseph as a sex slave in prison. Zuleika would then be able to have her way with him whenever she wanted, away from the prying eyes of the rest of the court.

There is a fascinating midrash on Psalm 146 that deals with this. Apparently, Mrs. Potiphar used to come to the prison to try and seduce Joseph even during the two years he was in jail.

> *When the wicked woman came she would torture him with words. She would say: I have had you put in prison. He said to her:* The Lord frees those that are bound up. *(Ps. 146:7) She said to him: I will pluck out your eyes [If you don't sleep with me]. He said to her:* The Lord gives sight to the blind. *(Ps. 146:8) She said to him: I will bring low your posture [bend you over for sex]. He said:* The Lord straightens those bent low. *(Ps 146:8) (b. Yoma 35b)*

This notion of not just Mrs. Potiphar but also all the women of Egypt instantly becoming smitten with Joseph is supported by the midrashic commentary on Jacob's blessing of Joseph. In Jacob's dying words to Joseph he says: *ben porat Yosef ben porat ale ayin banot tsaadah ale shur*, which is commonly translated as: "Joseph is a fruitful bough, a fruitful bough by a spring; his branches run over the wall" (Gen 49:22). This is a bit too certain-sounding in English for an essentially incomprehensible Hebrew phrase.[4] Rather than fruitful boughs, some have seen wild donkeys, and rather than climbing branches, wild asses.[5] There

---

4. Kugel, *In Potiphar's House*, 85.
5. On wild donkeys, see Gen 16:2; A.B. Ehrlich, *Randglossen zur hebräischen Bibel*, vol. 1, *Genesis–Exodus* (Leipzig, 1908), 250, as mentioned in Kugel, *In Potiphar's House*, 1990. On wild asses, see E. A. Speiser, *Genesis*, AB (Garden City, NY: Doubleday, 1964), 367–68, as mentioned in Kugel, *In Potiphar's House*.

is another reading, though, which takes *banot* simply as "girls" and reads the third clause separately: "Girls walk [climb] upon a wall."[6] Why? To see Joseph! About this Targum Pseudo-Jonathan says: "And when the [Egyptians] praised you [Joseph], the daughters of the rulers would walk along the walls and cast down in front of you bracelets and golden ornaments so that you might look at them." [7]

Indeed, this is a very early tradition, as Jerome in the fourth century CE writes: "O Joseph, I say, you who are so handsome that the whole throng of Egyptian girls looked down from the walls and towers and windows."[8] Joseph even meets his Egyptian wife in such a manner in the classic Joseph and Aseneth. "Joseph said to Pentephres, 'Who is this woman [Aseneth] who is standing on the upper floor by the window? Let her leave this house,' because Joseph was afraid, saying, 'This one must not molest me too.' . . . And all the wives and daughters of the Egyptians, when they saw Joseph, suffered badly because of his beauty."[9] In this rather shocking story of Joseph first seeing the woman he will marry, and the mother of Ephraim and Manasseh, we are told again of the inability of Egyptian women to control themselves when they see Joseph's legendary beauty. This assertion goes squarely against some of the major assumptions in purity culture: that only men, not women, are visually stimulated, and that men want sex, while women endure it.

The rabbis imagine a racist and classist society in Egypt in which Zuleika's female peers were shocked and embarrassed by her desiring a Hebrew slave and probably even more so by *his* rejection of *her*. The

---

6. Kugel, *In Potiphar's House*, 86. Kugel cites Marcus Jastrow, *A Dictionary of the Targumim, the Talmud Bavli and Yerushalmi and the Midrashic Literature* (Peabody, MA: Hendrickson, 1967), *ad loc.*, saying: "cf. the Arabic cognate *sa'ida* 'rise, climb.'" That this can be the sense of the D-form of the verb in Aramaic is suggested.

7. Kugel, *In Potiphar's House*, 87.

8. Jerome, *S. Hieronymi Presbyteri Opera*, CCSL 72 (Turnholt: Brepols, 1949), 56.

9. C. Burchard, trans., "Joseph and Aseneth," *OTP* 2:210.

imagined social pressure on Mrs. Potiphar was intense. Accordingly, Zuleika sought to demonstrate to the other Egyptian women that the problem was not her desire to flaunt the racism and class distinctions of her society but simply that Joseph's powerful sexual attractiveness transcended racial boundaries. But if the rabbis imagine all Egyptian women as unable to control themselves around Joseph, they also have serious questions about how and whether Joseph used his agency, power, and sexuality in this scenario.

Men's Incredulity at Sexual Refusal

The rabbis, it must be said, are extremely skeptical of the possibility of women raping men, as depicted earlier in their understanding of Lot and his daughters. Almost no attention is paid to the danger Zuleika poses to Joseph's body or sexual preferences. Rabbinic interpretation focuses instead on Joseph resisting temptation. Some of the rabbis go so far as to blame Joseph for his difficult situation with Zuleika. Their blame falls into two broad categories: Joseph is either too pretty or too prideful.

The rabbis imagine Joseph publicly practicing a certain amount of female-coded vanity and blame him for inciting the Egyptian women to desire him.[10] "His master's wife cast her eyes upon Joseph" (Gen 39:7 KJV). What is written before this passage? "And Joseph was beautiful of form, and fair to look upon" (39:6, my translation). "A man was standing in the market, penciling his eyes, curling his hair and lifting his heel. He said 'I am handsome, and I am strong, I am a handsome hero.' They [people in the market] said to him, if you are a hero, and if you are strong, there is a bear upon you, rise and attack!" (Gen. Rab. 87:3, my translation).

The rabbis imagine Joseph penciling his eyes (a common practice across genders in Egypt) but also curling his Asiatic hair (in Egyptian art, men usually have their hair cut short or shaved). The lifting of the

---

10. Kugel, *In Potiphar's House*, 78.

heel is probably best understood as a euphemism for showing off what was under the short men's skirt, the *shendyt*, that would have been his normal attire. The rabbis imagine Joseph making himself a sexually alluring target, and they use the words of the people in the market to mock Joseph's inability to defend himself from the possibility of female rape by comparing it to a bear attack.

The rabbis simply cannot imagine an attractive young man turning down sex on his own. They imagine a supernatural intervention is the only way a seventeen-year-old in the prime of life could turn down an invitation to sexual intercourse, even if it was adultery that would endanger his life if he was caught.

> And it came to pass after these things *(Gen 39:7) It is written:* For the rod [shevet] of wickedness shall not rest upon the lot of the righteous *(Ps. 125:3)*. . . . *Rabbi Yitzhak said: There is no rest for him [the righteous] along the company of the wicked, but only along the company of the righteous. Why?* That the righteous will not put their hands into iniquity *(Ps 125)*. Another word [interpretation]: For the rod of the wicked *applies to Potiphar's wife*. Shall not rest upon the lot of the righteous *applies to Joseph. (Gen. Rab. 87:2, my translation)*

The rabbis imagine Zuleika as the *shevet* (probably best understood here as a member of a tribe rather than as a literal rod) that is not allowed to rest on the righteous Joseph, lest he, ahem, "put his hands into iniquity." Thus, according to rabbinic logic, it was only God who prevented Joseph from positively responding to Zuleika's advances rather than any sense of propriety or sexual agency on Joseph's part.

Interpretive history imagines Joseph as a sort of desirous victim who was really "asking for it." The rabbis imagine that in the womb of his mother, Joseph began life as a female fetus. When Leah was praying for her seventh male fetus to become a girl, so that Rachel could have at least as many boys as the handmaids, she also prayed for

Rachel's womb to be opened (b. Ber. 60a). Rachel indeed became pregnant, with a girl! So, Leah, along with Zilpah and Bilhah, prayed that Rachel's girl would become a boy, and their prayer was answered (Gen. Rab. 72:6). Targum Pseudo-Jonathan goes even further, collapsing the time frame to say that Leah prayed and the fetuses in her and Rachel's wombs switched souls and sex organs. Dinah, originally conceived in Rachel's womb, came to Leah, and Joseph, originally conceived in Leah's womb, came to Rachel (Targum Jonathan on Gen 30:21). Even before Joseph was born, he was classified as an *androginus* or having a multisexed potentiated-body, one of the six genders (albeit based on physical sexual characteristics) discussed in rabbinic writings.[11]

In her masterwork *The Beginning of Desire*, Avivah Zornberg notes that this sort of extra genderedness is implicit in his name, saying, "Indeed, the word for 'excess'—*hosafa*—is another form of the root of Joseph's name."[12] Male-sexed and male-gender-performing Joseph will ever after have some extra femininity that he will use to be even more attractive. Wendy Zierler also wonders at Joseph's perpetual sexual nonconformity, especially in light of biblical and rabbinic portrayals of Egyptian hypersexuality (Ezek 23:20; b. Sotah 13b; Midrash Tanhuma on Gen 39:7):

> *Was Joseph, the product of his father's privileged love [and gender transgressive clothing], a kind of perpetual innocent, incapable of reading conventional, social-sexual cues? Might he have innocently mistaken Potiphar's wife's interests and advances as playful banter . . . ? Was she perhaps humiliated*

---

11. Sarah Freidson, "More than Just Male and Female: The Six Genders in Ancient Jewish Thought," Sefaria, 2021, https://www.sefaria.org/sheets/37225?lang=bi. For usage of these terms over time, see Elliot Kukla, "Terms for Gender Diversity in Classical Jewish Texts," TransTorah, 2006, http://www.transtorah.org/PRDs?CLassical_Jewish_Terms_for_Gender_Diversity.pdf.

12. Avivah Gottlieb Zornberg, *The Beginning of Desire: Reflections on Genesis* (New York: Doubleday, 1995), 267.

by his innocent rebuff? Did she view him, in his exaggerated [hosafa] beauty and chastity, as a kind of manipulative tease? Was he blind to the effects of his behavior and identity performance?[13]

Indeed, Joseph's performance of gender was a study in excess beauty and youthful naivete. Joseph's attractiveness crossed gender boundaries and drew on his prebirth sex swap, his father intentionally clothing him in the material culture of a young woman (his mother!) to whom Jacob was sexually attracted, and his youthful coquettishness. Even Chrysostom points out that Egyptian women were "under the spell" of Joseph's beauty.[14]

Joseph being too attractive and too sexually available was not the only flaw that the rabbis see as cause for Joseph's situation with Mrs. Potiphar. In the context of early midrash, that Joseph experiences torment in Egypt and winds up in prison is neither the doing of the Potiphars nor of Joseph himself but of God as retribution for Joseph's earlier vanity and pride. As we see in Genesis Rabbah, Joseph is the young man without understanding who is caught up in the guiles of Mrs. Potiphar:

> And it came to pass after these things *(Gen 39:7) It is written* And I beheld among the thoughtless ones *(Prov. 7:7)* Pethaim *alludes to the tribal ancestors. Rabbi Levi said, "In Arabia a youth is called* 'fante'" *(thoughtless)*. I discovered among the youths a young man void of understanding *(Prov 7:7) This is Joseph. He was void of understanding in that he slandered [*lshon hra: *proscribed in Num 14:36 and Prov 10:18] against his brothers. Is there any greater lack of understanding than this? And he went down to Egypt. And*

---

13. Zierler, "Joseph(ine), the Singer," 102.
14. Mark Sheridan, ed., *Genesis 12–50*, Ancient Christian Commentary on Scripture (Downers Grove, IL: InterVarsity, 2002), 250.

> behold, there met him a woman *(Prov 7:10) this is Potiphar's wife*. With the attire of a harlot *for Joseph*. And wily of heart *towards her husband*. She is riotous and rebellious *she goes about crying*. Her feet abide not in her house *but:* Now she is in the streets, now in the broad places *asking and saying, "Have you seen Joseph?"* So she caught him and kissed him. She caught him by his garment *(Gen 39:11)* She looked impudently at him *(Prov 7:13)*—Saying: Lie with me *(Gen 39:11)*. (Gen. Rab. 87:1, my translation)

The rabbis understand that Joseph was introduced to Mrs. Potiphar as the literal embodiment of the adulterous woman from Proverbs 7, specifically because of his prideful yet clueless slandering of his brothers. But perhaps it was not just thoughtlessness that landed Joseph into hot water. As is pointed out later in the same midrashic collection, Joseph's punishments fit his crimes.

> His master's wife cast her eyes upon Joseph *(Gen 39:7)*. *Therefore listen to me, you men of understanding: Far be it from God that he should do wickedness (Job 34:10). What is the workmanship of the Holy One, Blessed be He? For the work of man he will require and cause every man to find his ways (ib 11)*. Rabbi Meir, Rabbi Judah and Rabbi Simeon. *And Joseph brought an evil report of them (Gen 37:2)*. Rabbi Meir said: [commenting on what the evil report might be] Your children are suspect of eating limbs torn from a living animal. Rabbi Judah said: They insult the sons of the bondmaids and call them slaves. Rabbi Simeon said: They cast their eyes on the daughters of the country. Rabbi Judah in [the name of] Rabbi Simeon said: To the three: *A just balance and scale are the Lord's (Prov. 16:11)*. The Holy One, Blessed be He, said to him [Joseph]: You said, "Your sons are suspect of eating limbs torn from a living animal." By your life, even the in the act of wickedness,

> *they slaughter ritually.* And they slaughtered a he-goat *(Gen 32:31).* You said: *They insult the sons of the bondmaids and call them slaves.* Joseph was sold for a slave *(Ps. 105:17).* You said: *They cast their eyes on the daughters of the land. I will incite a bear against you.* His master's wife cast her eyes. *(Gen. Rab. 87:3, my translation)*

Just as Joseph spoke against his brothers, accusing them of consuming forbidden blood, calling them slaves, and engaging in unauthorized sex, so was blood used in the ploy to sell him, so did Joseph himself became a slave, and so he was tempted to engage in forbidden sex.

The rabbis quoted above simply do not understand Joseph as a moral exemplar and certainly not as a victim. Instead, when Zuleika tormented him with repeated commands to commit adultery, the rabbis understand that Joseph was receiving the just rewards based on oversexualizing himself and being too prideful.

How many times are these the modern tactics for blaming the victim of rape? "What were you wearing?" "You brought this on yourself." "If only you didn't act so stuck up and talked to them, they would have left you alone." Not much has changed in responses to rape in the last several centuries. Further, according to the interpretation above, at least some rabbis cannot conceive of a young man who would turn down sexual intimacy, even with the possible threat of retributive execution if he were discovered, without divine aid. However, while this attitude toward voracious male sexuality may have been common in the rabbis, at least one biblical character seems to understand Joseph as a moral exemplar and unwilling victim.

Potiphar's Incredulity at Joseph's Betrayal: An Unoffended Husband

When Mrs. Potiphar tells her tale (the fivefold repetition of the root *debar* ["speak"] in vv. 17 and 19 in addition to *amar* ["say"] suggests that she is multiplying words),[15] to *Joseph's master*, the text says that Potiphar is furious. But it does not say *at whom*. There is very good reason to think Potiphar is furious at his duplicitous wife.

As a response to his wife's words, Potiphar takes Joseph and *gives* him to the prison. Potiphar certainly would be within his rights to have a slave who attempted to rape his wife executed. Instead, Potiphar commits him to prison. This is not just any prison for riffraff but the prison where the king's prisoners are kept, and these prisoners are treated well enough that they are sometimes released and returned to the presence of the king (Gen 40:21). Not only is Joseph in the nicest prison, but the prison is in Potiphar's household.

Potiphar continues to interact with Joseph and entrust matters into his care. Remember that Potiphar is Pharaoh's captain of the guard (39:1). It is precisely this same captain of the guard in whose house is the prison (40:3, 7; 41:10) and who still gives Joseph assignments directly (40:4). There is now another layer of management between Joseph and Potiphar in the person of the prison house chief (39:21–23). But Potiphar would have been well aware of *his* prison running smoothly (39:22–23) because of the work of his favorite servant.

In other words, instead of killing or even selling the slave who was accused of attempting to rape his wife, Potiphar simply moves Joseph to an area of his household with another layer of supervision so that Zuleika can no longer approach him. It seems that Potiphar only imprisons Joseph to keep him out of reach of Zuleika, rather than because Potiphar thinks Joseph did anything wrong.

Possible Prevention

In thinking through the story of Joseph and Mrs. Potiphar as a biblical case study for a woman sexually harassing and attempting to rape a man, it is important not only to think about what has gone wrong,

---

15. Sarna, *Genesis*, 275.

and the parallels in contemporary life, but what could have been better, both in terms of prevention and remediation, that also could be echoed in contemporary life.

Certainly, an initial issue that is prompted by the biblical text is that Potiphar does not seem to have been responding to the emotional-sexual needs of Mrs. Potiphar. The text is explicit that the only thing Potiphar *knew*—let the reader understand—was his bread (Gen 39:6). One possible way to read the hinge verse "now it came about after these things" is to read this as a description of Potiphar's retirement from home life as much as a description of Joseph's attractiveness. Presumably Joseph had been serving in Potiphar's home for some time before God's blessing on all he undertook became apparent. Yet he was attractive the whole time. It is not for nothing that Paul counseled married people to have regular sexual intercourse, lest they burn with passion (1 Cor 7:2–5). One line of thinking suggests that Potiphar depriving his wife of sexual intimacy was a context—but not a cause—of her abuse of Joseph.

This interpretation can be deeply problematic, though, as the reverse idea—that women are to blame for not satisfying their man's needs—is often weaponized to excuse affairs. The presentation here in Genesis is extreme and borders on the comical. Potiphar, a eunuch, divests himself entirely from sexual life and "knows" only his food. Genesis repeatedly insists that women have sexual needs and rights, too (Leah and Tamar spring to mind), and when those needs are neglected, trouble ensues. At any rate, Zuleika wanted sex. And the object of her desire was not/no longer her husband but her husband's Hebrew slave.

Early Christian interpreters, too, seem to put blame on Potiphar for his lack of thoughtfulness, in this case based on the sociology of power dynamics. Ambrose, the fourth-century church father, notes, "It was not within the power of a mere servant not to be looked upon. The husband should have been on his guard against the roving eyes of his wife. If the husband had no fear in regard to his spouse, Joseph thought it to be evidence of her chastity, not the permissiveness of neglect."[16] In other words, Potiphar set Joseph up for failure, not only by ignoring his wife's sexual needs but then by doing nothing to warn or protect his handsome servant, who had no real power, as an enslaved person, to save himself from the machinations of his owner's wife. Again, simply being more in touch with his own household would have prevented, or at least made more difficult, Zuleika's attempts to rape Joseph. Yet none of these efforts were made. Mrs. Potiphar's sexual harassment of Joseph continued until the day he escaped her sexual assault, only to be imprisoned after her false accusations against him.

Conclusion

The story of Joseph and Zuleika offers an essential opportunity to read deeply a biblical text to examine traumatic abuse through lenses of ethnicity, class, gender, power and above all sexual violence. Its context in Genesis, as well as the laser focus and clarity on who is doing what to whom, challenges assumptions about the biblical period and today. Even when interpretative communities have great difficulty believing that someone is a victim, we must hold to the narrative truth of Scripture. Today that means demanding restitution from the Potiphars and Zuleikas of the world and working toward justice and healing for our present-day Josephs.

Implications for Ministry

After Zuleika's sexual assault against—and false claim of attempted rape by—Joseph, and Joseph's imprisonment by Potiphar, everyone involved needed some type of restitution and remediation. As the victim, I think Joseph needed a place of safety and to be believed. As I have argued, the Bible certainly leaves open the possibility that Potiphar believed Joseph and made partial restitution to him by offering

---

16. Sheridan, *Genesis 12–50*, 251.

Joseph a place of safety from Zuleika's harassment, albeit in Potiphar's household jail.

But jail was still jail. Joseph was not publicly exonerated. Instead, Joseph was thrown in jail by the man he refused to betray. Joseph's further loss of freedom and prestige, as a victim of attempted rape after already being enslaved, is galling. The church fathers try to interpret Joseph's loss of his clothing and being forced into prison as a mark of honor. Chrysostom opines about Joseph running away from Mrs. Potiphar without his clothing and then being tossed in jail naked: "One could see this remarkable man emerging, divested of his clothes but garbed in the vesture of chastity, as though escaping unharmed from some fiery furnace, not only not scorched by the flames but even more conspicuous and resplendent."[17] And yet, with his virtue intact, Joseph nonetheless was in prison, ostensibly for an act he did not commit. The victim was blamed and punished, while the perpetrator, if punished at all, did not seem to receive any social opprobrium for her acts. Potiphar could provide restitution for Joseph by freeing him from jail and publicly announcing that he believed and trusted his servant. For Joseph and in our own day, false accusations and speculations of wrongdoing are best countered publicly, and honor must be restored with a louder voice than that which pronounced shame.

Mrs. Potiphar must also publicly confess. Obviously, she should speak honestly about her sexual harassment and sexual assault, but also about her racist attempts to dehumanize her victim in the eyes of his coworkers and master after her assault failed to become the rape she intended. Twice Zuleika spoke about "this Hebrew" whom she accused her husband of bringing into the household to molest others when Joseph himself was the victim of molestation. This was a woman of the dominant racial group using stereotypes to make false accusations against a racial minority that put his life in danger after he refused her. Does this sound familiar? Remediation for Mrs. Potiphar would be for

---

17. Sheridan, *Genesis 12–50*, 253.

her to admit her racism and violence and try to make material restitution to Joseph. This, of course, would not be enough. She sexually assaulted him, besmirched his integrity, weaponized law enforcement, and suborned perjury. Material restitution can never be sufficient to cover for assault and false imprisonment. But at least for all of her lying and defaming, she could be made to tell the truth, as should all those who falsely accuse.

Finally, the interpretative communities who have produced the commentary discussed above owe Joseph restitution as well. In blaming the victim for being too pretty, too prideful, or simply incapable of refusing sex, interpretative communities have made it easier to do the same thing when women and men report sexual harassment and abuse. From the ancient past to the present, society needs to challenge automatic assumptions in cases of sexual violence about who *is in* danger and who *is a* danger.

Farewell

Thank you for faithfully journeying through so much gender-based and sexual trauma in Genesis. This has undoubtably been difficult at times. But these stories are here for us to learn from. I see myself in Sarah, hurting others when I acted out of my own hurt. I see myself in Jacob and Leah, just wanting to be loved for who I am. With whom do you resonate in these chapters? And how do their stories move you to healing and loving self and neighbor? Saint Irenaeus famously proclaimed: "The glory of God is the [fully] living human" (*Haer.* 4.20.7). These stories of humans experiencing trauma and moving toward abundant life and healing are a gift to us, if we will receive them, so that we can join them on the journey.

BIBLIOGRAPHY

Abasili, Alexander. "Seeing Tamar through the Prism of an African Woman: A Contextual Reading of Genesis 38." *OTE* 24, no. 3 (2011): 555–73.

Abu-Lughod, Lila. *Writing Women's Worlds: Bedouin Stories*. Berkeley: University of California Press, 2008.

Adelman, Rachel. "Seduction and Recognition in the Story of Judah and Tamar and the Book of Ruth." *Nashim: A Journal of Jewish Women's Studies and Gender Issues* 23, no. 1 (2012): 87–109.

Anderson, Francis. I. "The Socio-juridical Background of the Naboth Incident." *JBL* 85, no. 1 (1966): 46–57.

Angelou, Maya, bell hooks, and Melvin McLeod. "'There's No Place to Go but Up'—Bell Hooks and Maya Angelou in Conversation." Lion's Roar, January 1, 1998. https://www.lionsroar.com/theres-no-place-to-go-but-up/.

Bal, Mieke. "Metaphors He Lives By." *Semeia* 61 (1993): 185–207.

Bechtel, Lyn M. "The Development of Job: Mrs. Job as Catalyst." In *Feminist Companion to Wisdom Literature*, edited by A. Brenner, 201–22. Sheffield: Sheffield Academic, 1995.

Bell, Catherine. *Ritual Theory, Ritual Practice*. New York: Oxford University Press, 1992.

Boase, Elizabeth. "Fragmented Voices: Collective Identity and Traumatization in Lamentations." In *Bible through the Lens of Trauma*, edited by Elizabeth Boase and Christopher G. Frechette, 49–66. Atlanta: SBL Press, 2016.

Briggs, Charles L. *Competence in Performance: The Creativity of Tradition in Mexicano Verbal Art*. Philadelphia: University of Pennsylvania Press, 1988.

Brown, Kemone S-G. *When Rape Becomes Acceptable: Corrective Rape in Jamaica*. Kingston: Tamarind Hill Press, 2017.

Brown, William. *Wisdom's Wonder: Character, Creature and Crisis in the Bible's Wisdom Literature*. Grand Rapids: Eerdmans, 2014.

Brueggemann, Walter. *Genesis*. Atlanta: John Knox, 1982.
Burchard, C., trans. "Joseph and Aseneth." *OTP* 2:177–247.
Butler, Judith. *Gender Trouble: Feminism and the Subversion of Identity*. New York: Routledge, 1990.
Cooper, Alan. "The Sense of the Book of Job." *Prooftexts* 17, no. 3 (1997): 227–44.
Davis, Ellen F. *Getting Involved with God: Rediscovering the Old Testament*. Boston: Cowley, 2001.
Dube, Musa. "Dinah (Genesis 34) at the Contact Zone: 'Shall Our Sister Become a Whore?'" In *Feminist Frameworks and the Bible: Power, Ambiguity, and Intersectionality*, edited by Juliana Claassens and Carolyn Sharp, 39–58. London: Bloomsbury T&T Clark, 2017.
Ehrlich, A.B. *Randglossen zur hebräischen Bibel*. Vol. 1, *Genesis–Exodus*. Leipzig, 1908.
Everhart, Jane. "Women Who Love Women Reading Hebrew Bible Texts: About a Lesbian Biblical Hermeneutic." In *Feminist Interpretation of the Hebrew Bible in Retrospect*, vol. 2, *Social Locations*, edited by Suzanne Scholz, 188–204. Sheffield: Sheffield Phoenix, 2014.
Fewell, Danna Nolan, and David Gunn. "Tipping the Balance: Sternberg's Reader and the Rape of Dinah." *JBL* 110, no. 2 (1991): 193–211.
Fisch, Solomon. "Midrash Ha-Gadol." *EncJud* 14:186–87.
Fleishman, Jacob. "Shechem and Dinah—In Light of Non-biblical and Biblical Sources." *ZAW* 116 (2004): 12–32.
Fleuckiger, Joyce Burkhalter. *In Amma's Healing Room: Gender and Vernacular Islam in South Asia*. Bloomington: Indiana University Press, 2006.
Fox, Everett. *The Five Books of Moses*. New York: Schocken, 1997.
Freidson, Sarah. "More than Just Male and Female: The Six Genders in Ancient Jewish Thought." Sefaria, 2021. https://www.sefaria.org/sheets/37225?lang=bi.
Frymer-Kensky, Tikva. "Law and Philosophy: The Case of Sex in the Bible." In *Women in the Hebrew Bible: A Reader*, edited by Alice Bach, 293–304. New York: Routledge, 1999.
Gade, Anna. *Perfection Makes Practice: Learning, Emotion, and the Recited Qur'an in Indonesia*. Honolulu: University of Hawai'i Press, 2004.

Gafney, Wil. "Lot Sexually Manipulates His Two Daughters." The Torah.com, 2021. https://www.thetorah.com/article/lot-sexually-manipulates-his-two-daughters.

———. *Womanist Midrash: A Reintroduction to the Women of the Torah and the Throne*. Louisville: Westminster John Knox, 2017.

Gerstenberger, E. S. "*Anah*." In vol. 6 of *Theologisches Wörterbuch zum Alten Testament VI*, 252–53. Stuttgart: Kohlhammer, 1989.

Gilbert, Jack. "A Brief for the Defense." In *Refusing Heaven: Poems*, 3. New York: Knopf, 2005.

Graybill, Rhiannon. *Texts after Terror: Rape, Sexual Violence, and the Hebrew Bible*. New York: Oxford University Press, 2021.

Greenberger, Chaya. "Judah and Tamar: Self-Esteem Lost and (Partially) Redeemed." *JBQ* 48, no. 1 (2020): 23–32.

Herman, Judith Lewis. *Trauma and Recovery: The Aftermath of Violence—From Domestic Abuse to Political Terror*. New York: Basic Books, 2015.

Hunter-Gault, Charlayne. *Corrective Rape: Discrimination, Assault, Sexual Violence, and Murder against South Africa's L.G.B.T. Community*. Chicago: Agate Digital, 2015.

Hymes, Dell. *"In Vain I Tried to Tell You": Essays in Native American Ethnopoetics*. Philadelphia: University of Pennsylvania Press, 1986.

Janzen, J. Gerald. *Job*. Atlanta: John Knox, 1985.

Jastrow, Marcus. *A Dictionary of the Targumim, the Talmud Bavli and Yerushalmi and the Midrashic Literature*. Peabody, MA: Hendrickson, 1967.

Jauss, Hans Robert. *Toward an Aesthetic of Reception*. Translated by Timothy Bahti. Minneapolis: University of Minnesota Press, 1982.

Jerome. *S. Hieronymi Presbyteri Opera*. CCSL 72. Turnholt: Brepols, 1949.

Johnson, Michael. "Domestic Violence: It's Not about Gender—Or Is It?" *Journal of Marriage and Family* 67, no. 5 (2005): 1126–30.

Joseph, Alison L. "Who Is the Victim in the Dinah Story?" The Torah.com, 2017. https://www.thetorah.com/article/who-is-the-victim-in-the-dinah-story.

Kelso, Julie. "Reading the Silence of Women in Genesis 34." In *The Bible, Gender, and Sexuality: Critical Readings*, edited by

Rhiannon Graybill and Lynn R. Huber, 19–38. London: T&T Clark, 2021.

Koraan, René, and Allison Geduld. "'Corrective Rape' of Lesbians in the Era of Transformative Constitutionalism in South Africa." *Potchefstroom Electronic Law Journal* 18, no. 5 (2015): 1930–52.

Kugel, James L. *In Potiphar's House: The Interpretive Life of Biblical Texts*. San Francisco: Harper Collins, 1990.

Kukla, Elliot. "Terms for Gender Diversity in Classical Jewish Texts." TransTorah, 2006. http://transtorah.org/PDFs/Classical_Jewish _Terms_for_Gender_Diversity.pdf.

Landsman, Irene Smith. "Crisis of Meaning in Trauma and Loss." In *Loss of the Assumptive World: A Theory of Traumatic Loss*, edited by Jeffery Kauffman, 10–20. New York: Brunner-Routledge, 2002.

Lier, Gudrun Elisabeth. "Translating ברך in Job 2:9—A Functionalist Approach." *AcT* 38, no. 2 (2018): 105–22.

Linafelt, Tod. *Surviving Lamentations: Catastrophe, Lament, and Protest in the Afterlife of a Biblical Book*. Chicago: University of Chicago Press, 2000.

Maggi, Wynne. *Our Women Are Free: Gender and Ethnicity in the Hindukush*. Ann Arbor: University of Michigan Press, 2001.

Mann, Thomas. *Joseph and His Brothers*. Translated by H. T. Loew Porter. New York: Knopf, 1948.

Menakem, Resmaa. *My Grandmother's Hands: Racialized Trauma and the Pathway to Mending Our Hearts and Bodies*. Las Vegas: Central Recovery, 2017.

Mitchel, Christopher Wright. *The Meaning of BRK "To Bless" in the Old Testament*. SBLDS 95. Atlanta: Scholars Press, 1987.

Nahmanides. *Commentary on the Torah: Genesis*. Translated by Charles B. Chavel. New York: Shilo, 1971.

Niditch, Susan. "Genesis." In *Women's Bible Commentary*, 20th anniversary ed., 27–50. Louisville: Westminster John Knox, 2012.

O'Connor, Kelly E., Terri N. Sullivan, Katherine M. Ross, and Khiya J. Marshall. "'Hurt People Hurt People': Relations between Adverse Experiences and Patterns of Cyber and In-Person Aggression and Victimization among Urban Adolescents." *Aggressive Behavior* 47, no. 4 (July 2021): 483–92.

Ostriker, Alicia Suskin. *The Nakedness of Our Fathers: Biblical Visions and Revisions*. New Brunswick, NJ: Rutgers University Press, 1997.

Parker, Eve Rebecca. "The Virgin and the Whore—An Interreligious Challenge for Our Times: Exploring the Politics of Religious Belonging with Tamar." *The Ecumenical Review* 71, no. 5 (2019): 693–705.

Rabow, Jerry. *The Lost Matriarch: Finding Leah in the Bible and Midrash*. Philadelphia: Jewish Publication Society, 2014.

Reynolds, Dwight. *Heroic Poets, Poetic Heroes: The Ethnography of Performance in an Arabic Oral Epic Tradition*. Ithaca, NY: Cornell University Press, 1995.

Rohr, Richard. *A Spring within Us: A Book for Daily Meditations*. Albuquerque, NM: CAC, 2016.

Sacks, Jonathan. "Disguise." Mikketz, 2012–2013. https://rabbisacks.org/covenant-conversation-miketz-disguise/.

Sarna, Nahum. *Genesis*. JPS Torah Commentary. Philadelphia: Jewish Publication Society, 1989.

Scholz, Suzanne. *Rape Plots: A Feminist Cultural Study of Genesis 34*. New York: Peter Lang, 2000.

———. "Through Whose Eyes? A 'Right' Reading of Genesis 34." In *Genesis: A Feminist Companion to the Bible*, edited by Athalya Brenner, 150–71. Sheffield: Sheffield Academic, 1998.

Seow, C. L. *Job 1–21: Interpretation and Commentary*. Grand Rapids: Eerdmans, 2013.

Shemesh, Yael. "Rape Is Rape Is Rape: The Story of Dinah and Shechem [Genesis 34]." *ZAW* 119 (2007): 2–21.

Sheridan, Mark, ed. *Genesis 12–50*. Ancient Christian Commentary on Scripture. Downers Grove, IL: InterVarsity, 2002.

Spivak, Gayatri Chakravorty. "Can the Subaltern Speak?" In *Marxism and the Interpretation of Culture*, edited by Cary Nelson and Lawrence Grossberg, 271–313. Urbana: University of Illinois Press, 1988.

Stiebert, Johanna. *Fathers and Daughters in the Hebrew Bible*. Oxford: Oxford University Press, 1998.

Trible, Phyllis. *God and the Rhetoric of Sexuality*. Philadelphia: Fortress, 1979.

Warrior, Robert Allen. "A Native American Perspective: Canaanites, Cowboys, and Indians." In *Voices from the Margin: Interpreting the Bible in the Third World*, rev. and exp. 3rd ed., edited by R. S. Sugirtharajah, 235–41. Maryknoll, NY: Orbis, 2006.

Webber, Sabra Jean. *Romancing the Real: Folklore and Ethnographic Representation in North Africa*. Philadelphia: University of Pennsylvania Press, 1991.

Westermann, Claus. *Genesis 37–50: A Commentary*. Translated by John Scullion. Minneapolis: Augsburg, 1986.

Zierler, Wendy. "Joseph(ine), the Singer: The Queer Joseph and Modern Jewish Writers." *NASHIM: A Journal of Jewish Women's Studies and Gender Issues* 24 (2013): 97–119.

Zornberg, Avivah Gottlieb. *The Beginning of Desire: Reflections on Genesis*. New York: Doubleday, 1995.

INDEX

Abraham (Avram), 2, 3, 10–27, 29, 35, 37

Bathshua, 102–3, 116, 123

Dinah, 3, 6, 7, 13, 50, 62, 71–87, 89, 97–100, 130

Egypt, 3, 6, 10, 15–22, 24, 26, 45, 46, 48, 63, 64, 66–69, 113, 114, 120, 121, 123–28, 130, 131
Esau, 46, 48–54, 56, 57, 59, 61, 62, 68, 77, 109
ethnicity, 47, 113, 115, 123, 136

foreign(er), 3, 7, 11, 17, 29, 30, 34–36, 43, 44, 81, 82, 115, 119, 122, 123, 125

gender, 1, 2, 4–7, 26, 29, 33, 46–48, 53, 55, 63–66, 69, 83, 89, 107, 108, 115, 120, 122, 128, 130, 131, 136, 138

HaGar, 3, 6, 10, 11, 14, 15, 19–22, 24, 26–29
healing, 1, 3, 5–7, 9, 10, 24, 26–28, 42, 43, 47, 48, 68, 69, 76, 93, 100, 117, 119, 136, 138

Isaac, 12, 13, 22, 24, 26, 35, 45, 46, 49, 51–54, 59, 65, 68, 69, 114
Ishmael, 15, 19, 22, 24, 26, 27, 35

Jacob, 2, 3, 6, 33, 45–73, 77–84, 87, 89, 97, 108, 111, 114, 121, 126, 131, 138

Job, 7, 89–100, 132
Joseph, 2, 3, 6, 7, 33, 35, 45–48, 59, 63–70, 82, 84, 101, 111–15, 119–38
Judah, 3, 7, 46, 70, 101–17, 123

Leah, 2, 3, 6, 45–48, 50, 54–63, 67–71, 83–85, 97, 108, 109, 129, 130, 135, 138
Levi, 60, 73, 74, 79, 80, 87
Lot, 6, 12–15, 26, 29–44, 128

midrash, 4, 5, 25, 30, 53, 57, 66, 92, 97, 107, 117, 124–27, 130–32
minority, 6, 32, 86, 137

Potiphar (Mrs.), 35, 66, 68, 112, 113, 119–37

Qetenah (daughter of Lot), 30, 38–43

Rachel, 2, 3, 46, 50, 54, 56–65, 68, 83, 108, 121, 129, 130
reproduce/reproduction, 7, 20, 22, 27, 60, 62, 63, 101, 103–6, 110

Sarah (Sarai), 2, 3, 6, 10–29, 35, 138
sex(uality), 1, 2, 4–7, 10, 11, 14, 17, 18, 20, 21, 23, 26, 29–35, 39, 41–45, 47, 53, 54, 57–59, 61–63, 66, 68–70, 72–79, 81–86, 96, 101–13, 115–17, 119–31, 133–38

Shechem, 71–87, 97
Simeon, 60, 73, 74, 79, 80, 87

Tamar, 3, 6, 7, 45–48, 68, 70, 76, 101–17, 123, 135
trauma, 1–7, 9–10, 15, 18–22, 24, 26, 27, 29–31, 33, 34, 38, 40, 42–44, 47, 59, 60, 68, 72, 86, 87, 89, 90, 95, 97–101, 105, 113, 116, 117, 119, 136, 138

Zeqenah (daughter of Lot), 30, 38–43
Zuleika (wife of Potiphar), 119, 121–29, 133–37